"We'll find homes for them."

Teddy was kneeling by the box full of kittens. The kittens were tumbling all over themselves, playing with his fingers.

"Dad, maybe we could. . . ."

"Yes, Dad! Just for a little while," Val put in.

"Ye gods!" Doc groaned. "We have a cat, two dogs, four rabbits, hamsters, a duck, and Teddy's chickens, and you're asking me to take in kittens?"

"Not forever," Val said quickly. "Just until we can find someone to adopt them. And they're so cute and cuddly, I bet we'll find homes for them real fast."

ANIMAL INN

ADOPT-A-PET

Virginia Vail

AN
APPLE
PAPERBACK

SCHOLASTIC INC.
New York Toronto London Auckland Sydney

ISBN 0-590-43431-4

Copyright © 1987 by Cloverdale Press. All rights reserved.
Published by Scholastic Inc. APPLE PAPERBACKS
is a registered trademark of Scholastic Inc.

12 11 10 9 8 7 6 5 4 3 2 1   9/8 0 1 2 3/9

Printed in the U.S.A.

First Scholastic printing, June 1987

ADOPT-A-PET

Chapter 1

It was a peaceful night in late spring, and everyone in the big stone house on Old Mill Road was sound asleep. Valentine Taylor was curled up around the soft, furry body of Cleveland, her cat, and having a lovely dream. She was riding The Gray Ghost across a field, her long chestnut hair streaming behind her in the breeze. The dapple-gray gelding was approaching a high stone wall, but Val wasn't in the least afraid, because in the dream, The Ghost was young again and the cataracts that now dimmed his vision had disappeared as if by magic. He soared into the air as though he had wings and cleared the wall with room to spare like the champion jumper he'd once been. Suddenly the field turned into a show ring, and thousands of people were cheering as Val slowed The Ghost to a trot and came to the center of the ring. A lady in a blue dress fastened a purple rosette to his bridle and handed Val an enormous silver trophy. Val was so proud, she thought she'd explode. The cheering and applause got louder, and now bells were ringing as well, to celebrate The Ghost's victory. Bells. . . .

Rrrrinnngg!

Val opened first one eye, then the other. A bell *was* ringing. It was the telephone in the hall outside her bedroom door. Val squinted at her bedside clock. Ten forty-five. She was used to late-night calls — her father's animal patients didn't always choose the most convenient times to get sick or to give birth, and since Val was going to be a veterinarian like Doc Taylor when she grew up, she understood that a vet was always on call. Who could it be this time? Had Mrs. Williams' dachshund started having her puppies? Mrs. Williams was terribly nervous about Fritzi's first litter, and both Val and Doc had been anticipating something like this.

Clutching Cleveland, she sat up groggily, swung her legs over the side of the bed, and headed for the door. But as she opened it, she heard her father's voice.

"Yes, this is Doctor Taylor. . . . No, I wasn't asleep. . . . That's an emergency, all right! I'll be there as soon as I can — about fifteen minutes."

"Dad?"

Val stuck her head into the hall, fully awake now. "Is it Fritzi Williams? Are the puppies coming?"

Doc shook his head. "No, that was George Frick, the caretaker at the Humane Society animal shelter.

2

One of the kennels is on fire and it's spreading to the cattery. He's called the fire department and they're on their way. Some of the animals are in bad shape — I have to get over there right away."

Val dropped Cleveland and dashed into her room to find her clothes. "I'm coming with you!" she called over her shoulder. The thought of all those cats and dogs, kittens and puppies that might be losing their lives at that very moment was horrifying. Doc Taylor was on the board of the Essex Humane Society, so Val knew how overcrowded the shelter was and how badly they needed more space to house all the homeless animals the Society cared for. They had been trying for years to raise enough money to build a new shelter, and in the meantime the old one had become horribly overcrowded.

When Val emerged from her room a few minutes later in jeans and flannel shirt, she saw her eleven-year-old sister Erin standing in the hall, rubbing her eyes.

"What's going on?" Erin asked sleepily.

"It's okay, Erin," Val assured her, gently leading her back to her room. "Get into bed. Dad and I are going to the Humane Society shelter — there's a fire. We'll take care of everything, don't worry."

"A fire?" Erin repeated. "Oh, Vallie, that's dreadful!"

"I know," Val said, tucking Erin in. "But Dad's

the best vet in the world, and he'll know just what to do. Go back to sleep, Erin. We won't be gone long.''

"I won't be able to sleep a wink,'' Erin mumbled, but her eyes were already closing.

Val tiptoed out, closing Erin's door behind her. She knew she didn't have to worry about her little brother, Teddy. Teddy slept like a log; nothing ever woke him up.

"Vallie? You coming?'' Doc called from downstairs.

"Yes, Dad. Right now!'' Val called back softly, struggling into a sweat shirt. Even though it was May, the night air was chilly.

Sunshine, the Taylors' golden retriever, followed her down the stairs, whimpering. Val knew that Jocko, the little shaggy black and white mongrel, would be sound asleep under Teddy's bed. She patted Sunshine on the head and told him to stand guard as she ran out to the driveway where Doc had already started the van. Val climbed into the passenger seat and fastened her seat belt. Doc backed out of the driveway and drove down the deserted street.

Val leaned forward, peering through the night. "Can't you go a little faster, Dad?'' she asked anxiously.

"I could, but I won't,'' Doc said. "It won't do any good to those poor animals if we have an accident on the way." He glanced over at Val. "I shouldn't have let you come with me," he added with a sigh. "But I'll need all the help I can get, and you're the best assistant I've got."

Val felt a warm glow of pride that helped to loosen the knot of fear in her stomach.

"I don't need all that much sleep," she said. "And besides, tomorrow's Sunday, so I can sleep late. And you know I couldn't have stayed in bed when I could be helping you take care of those dogs and cats. Oh, I hope none of them have died!"

"I do, too, Vallie," Doc said. "From what George told me on the phone, he smelled smoke and opened all the pens immediately. Most of the animals ran out, and he carried the ones that were too frightened or confused to move. But those old buildings are like so much tinder — they must have gone up like a bonfire. We'll have our work cut out for us, honey. Just keep your head, and don't get all emotional on me."

"I won't, I promise," Val said quickly. "If I'm going to be a vet like you, I have to learn to be calm when there's an emergency. And I will be, honest!"

Doc reached out and squeezed her hand. "I know you will. Don't know what I'd do without you. Sometimes I forget that you're only thirteen."

Val returned the squeeze. "I may be only thirteen, but I'm big for my age, and I *feel* a lot older."

As they approached the animal shelter, Val heard the fire sirens, and a moment later she saw a dull red glow in the sky. Doc pulled up next to one of the fire engines, and he and Val leaped out of the van, heading for the shelter's main building. The red glow had turned into an orange blaze. The fire engines' hoses were pouring water on the fire, and someone was shouting instructions over a bullhorn. Frantic dogs ran around in circles, barking at the top of their lungs. Val almost tripped over a terrified cat that dashed between her legs in the direction of the trees beyond the area where the fire raged. Looking up, she saw flames reflected in the wide eyes of other cats that had raced up into the branches for safety. Doc, carrying his black bag, strode over to a tall, lean man whose face was blackened with smoke. The man was holding a limp bundle of fur in his arms.

"Calico," the man said, shoving the bundle at Doc. "She just had kittens. They're over there. . . ." He jerked his head in the direction of the woods. "They're okay, but Calico's in bad shape. And then there's Boxer. . . . I'll show you."

Doc took the terrified cat from the man's arms, and she opened her mouth and let out an agonized squall. Val saw, in the flickering firelight, that most of her fur had been burned off.

6

"I'll take Calico, Dad," she said. "You take care of Boxer."

The cat mewed pitifully as Val snuggled her close to her chest, murmuring soothing words. She couldn't help thinking of Cleveland, her own cat. If something like this had happened to Cleveland, she wouldn't have been able to stand it.

Doc thrust a tube of ointment into her hand.

"Put this on Calico's burns," he said. "Find the kittens. Calico will feel better if she has her family around her." He turned to the tall, thin man. "George, where's Boxer?"

He loped off after George Frick, and Val began to cover Calico with the burn ointment. Calico wasn't grateful for the attention. She screeched at the top of her lungs and tried to claw Val, but Val managed to calm her down with soothing words, stroking what remained of the cat's singed fur. Tiny mews guided her to where the newborn kittens huddled in a box at the base of a huge oak tree, and Val put Calico down with her babies.

"Here's your family, Calico," she said. "They're just fine, see? And you will be, too, in a little while. We'll take you all to Animal Inn. Don't worry, you'll like your new home."

Calico seemed to forget her burns as she tended to her five wailing babies, licking them thoroughly one after the other.

"Valentine Taylor! Is that you?" A brisk, clear voice carried over the crackle of the flames and the roar of the fire engines, and Val looked up to see an extremely odd-looking figure striding in her direction. Lit from behind by the light of the fire, it looked like a Halloween witch. Strands of hair blew every which way from an untidy knot on top of its head, and long, bony arms swung purposefully in rhythm with its pace. The figure was wearing what looked like a man's shirt tucked into wide, floppy trousers secured midway down the legs with bicycle clips. Val grinned in spite of herself. Everyone knew Miss Maggie Rafferty, a pillar of the Essex Humane Society and even more of an animal nut than Val was herself. Miss Maggie admitted to being eighty-two years old, but some people in town said she lied about her age. She was probably closer to ninety, but she had the energy of a woman less than half her age — whatever it was.

"Yes, it's me, Miss Maggie," Val said. "Doc let me come along to help him take care of the animals."

"Young Theodore must be out of his mind," Miss Maggie said with a snort. "This is no place for children!"

She stood over Val, hands on hips, bright blue eyes sparkling with indignation. Then she caught sight of Calico and her kittens, and her expression softened. "Why, that's Calico, isn't it? I'd know her anywhere, even without most of her fur. I found her in front of Schneider's Grocery Store three weeks ago and brought her here myself. The kittens all right?"

"They're fine," Val said. "And Calico will be, too, when her burns heal and her fur grows back. I put antibiotic ointment on her — the burns aren't really all that bad."

"Okay, I'll take 'em," Miss Maggie said.

Val stared at her. "What do you mean?" she asked.

"Are you deaf, girl? I said I'd take 'em! You just give me some of that ointment, and Calico and the kittens can stay with me until we find them good homes."

"But, Miss Maggie, you already have ten cats . . ." Val began, but Miss Maggie cut her off.

"Eleven, and three dogs. Can't keep them forever, you know, but this is an emergency, right?"

Val nodded.

"Got an enormous house with nobody in it but me," Miss Maggie continued. "No reason why I can't take in some of these poor creatures. I like animals better than people, anyway — most people, that is. Your father's an exception. Reminds me of a dog I used to have — Airedale. Real smart, that dog was. Young Theodore's smart, too." She leveled her intent blue gaze at Val. "You look like him."

Trying not to giggle, Val said, "My father or the Airedale?"

"Both!" snapped Miss Maggie. "Well, if you're here to help, why aren't you helping? Calico's not going anywhere. Come on! There are lots of other animals that need attention!"

She stretched out a hand and grabbed Val's in a surprisingly strong grip, pulling her to her feet.

"Catch that dog!" Miss Maggie bellowed, as a terrified spaniel dashed past them, heading for the woods.

Val obediently lunged for the dog, but Miss Maggie beat her to it, tackling the animal and bringing it to the ground. After a brief tussle, which Val watched, astounded, Miss Maggie sat up, holding the spaniel in her arms.

"This one looks all right to me — just scared, is all. I'll take him, too. Find me a rope, Valentine, and tie him to that tree. I'll pick him up later."

Val hurried off in search of a rope, and found one in the vet van. She and Miss Maggie tied the dog securely, and it was so stunned that it didn't even yelp.

"Vallie!" She heard Doc calling her, and ran in the direction of his voice. When she reached him, he was tending to a large mixed breed suffering from burns and what appeared to be a broken leg.

"A beam fell on him," Doc told her. "Hold him while I give him a shot of painkiller. Where's that ointment?"

"In my pocket," Val said, pulling out the tube. After Doc had administered the shot, she very gently smoothed the ointment on the dog's burned skin.

"This one has to go to Animal Inn," Doc said. "Don't have time to set that leg right now. Help me carry him to the van, Vallie."

Together, they lifted the big dog and laid him gently on a bed of blankets in the vet van, next to another injured dog and two groggy cats. The animals were all either burned or otherwise hurt, and Val blinked back tears of compassion.

"You'd better stay here with our patients, Vallie," Doc said. "Keep them calm and quiet if you can. I'm afraid there'll be more before the night is over."

Though Val wanted to be at Doc's side, taking care of the other injured animals, she knew that she was needed where she was, so she stayed in the van, stroking the dogs and cats and murmuring soothing words.

When the vet van was filled to capacity, Doc returned. He looked exhausted, but he was smiling.

"We didn't lose a single one," he said happily. "And it's all due to George Frick. He's the hero of this disaster. If he hadn't smelled smoke when the fire first started and opened all the pens, I don't like to think what might have happened."

"How's Miss Maggie going to take home all those animals she's going to take care of?" Val asked. "She can't put them in the basket of her bicycle!"

"Miss Maggie." Doc shook his head in amusement. "She's something else! She cornered poor George Frick and got him to say he'd drive them to her house. Miss Maggie is a wonder."

"She sure is," Val said. Tired as she was, and sad as she was about the injured animals, she couldn't help smiling. "She told me you reminded her of an Airedale she used to have. And then she said that I looked like you — and the Airedale!"

"Woof," Doc said, smiling, too. "As far as I'm concerned, you don't look like anybody but you, and I wouldn't have it any other way." He looked at her closely then. "But you do look tired, honey. Suppose I drop you off at the house? Mike can help me unload our new patients at Animal Inn." Mike Strickler worked nights at Doc Taylor's veterinary clinic.

Val shook her head. "You're just as tired as I am," she said. "And we can both sleep late tomorrow, remember? I'm fine, Dad, honest. We'll get everything done a lot faster if there are three of us instead of two."

Doc started the engine and turned the van around, heading back to the main road. "Don't know what

12

I'd do without you, Vallie. . . . I wonder how many times I've said that over the past few years?"

Val smiled. "Lots." She felt both proud and sad. Three years ago her mother had died in an automobile accident. Val tried very hard to take her place as much as possible, taking care of Doc, Teddy, and Erin. With the help of Mrs. Racer, the Taylors' housekeeper, the family had overcome their grief and gone on with their lives. But deep down inside, they all missed her very much.

As if he had read Val's thoughts, Doc said, "Your mother would be very proud of you . . . of all three of you."

"All *four* of us," Val said. "She'd be proud of you, too."

They drove in silence through the night for a few minutes. Then Val said, "Miss Maggie's a real character, isn't she, Dad?"

"Indeed she is," Doc agreed. "She may look a little strange, and she certainly doesn't hesitate to say what she thinks, so many people make fun of her. But her mind's as sharp as yours or mine, and she loves animals as if they were the children she never had. You hear a lot about 'a heart of gold.' Well, Miss Maggie really has one. When she was my third-grade teacher, I was scared to death of her, but as I got older I found out what a fine person she really is."

"Maybe I'll be like Miss Maggie when I get old," Val said, stifling a yawn. "Because I love animals, too, and I'm never going to get married. I'll be too busy being a vet." She snuggled closer to Doc. "Maybe I'll be a character, too. . . ."

That made Doc chuckle. "You might change your mind — about not getting married, I mean," he said. "It's not something you have to decide right away."

But Val didn't reply. She had fallen fast asleep.

Chapter
2

When Val woke up the next morning, bright sunshine was streaming across her bed, and Cleveland was curled up in his usual place beside her. Val blinked and sat up. She didn't remember coming home, getting undressed and into her pajamas, or climbing into bed. The last thing she recalled was sitting next to Doc in the vet van on the way to Animal Inn, talking about Miss Maggie Rafferty. . . .

"Oh, no!" she groaned aloud, causing Cleveland to open one yellow eye and give her a curious stare. "I must have fallen asleep in the van, and Dad had to put me to bed like a little kid! Fine assistant I am."

Cleveland yawned widely and rolled over onto his back, silently inviting Val to tickle his tummy. She rubbed the soft orange and white fur automatically, feeling very ashamed of herself. She'd been so eager to help Doc and Mike, and she'd pooped out, that's what she'd done.

"Oh, Cleveland." She sighed. "How am I ever

going to be a good vet if I can't even stay awake in an emergency?"

Cleveland only purred, but Val kept talking to him anyway.

"Cleveland, you're a very lucky cat, do you know that?" she said. "Imagine if you'd been abandoned by your family, or never had a family at all, and were living in the animal shelter, and it burned down. You might have had all your beautiful fur burned off, like Calico. You might even have *died*! Only none of the animals in the shelter died last night, thank goodness. And we took the badly injured ones to Animal Inn — or Dad did."

Rrrooowww, said Cleveland, grabbing Val's hand with his paws and taking a little bite of her fingers.

"Ouch!" said Val. "Watch it with those teeth!" She sniffed the air.

"You know, I can still smell burning wood. . . ." She sniffed again, then took a strand of her hair and held it under her nose. "It's me! I smell like hickory-smoked bacon. Guess I better take a shower. And then I'll go down and fix breakfast for Dad and Teddy and Erin — yes, and for you, too."

Val always made a big breakfast for the family on Sunday mornings, usually pancakes and sausage. She looked at her bedside clock. Ten o'clock! They must be starving!

Before Val could get out of bed, her door burst open. Jocko and Sunshine galloped into the room, tails wagging, and tongues hanging out. Both dogs stood up on their hind legs, their front paws on her bed. Cleveland looked annoyed, sat up, and began washing his already spotless fur, as Val patted first one head, then the other.

"Good morning, sleepyhead."

Doc came in, fully dressed and looking cheerful and rested. He'd even trimmed his beard, Val noticed. It had been a little scruffy yesterday.

"Get a good night's sleep?" he asked, sitting on the edge of her bed.

Val gave him a kiss. "Yes, I sure did. But, Dad, you should have woken me up last night when we got to Animal Inn. Did you and Mike find space for all our new patients?" she asked.

"Just barely," Doc said. "It's a little tight, but everybody has a place to rest. It was close to two o'clock when we finished. You were sleeping so peacefully, I didn't want to disturb you. You did a fine job, Vallie, and Mike and I were able to handle the rest."

"So you didn't really need me, huh?" Val said, a little sadly.

"As I said, we managed, but just barely. You'll have plenty to do later today. I'm going out there this afternoon, to make sure all our patients are doing well, and I'd like you to go with me."

"Me, too! Me, too!"

Teddy hurtled into Val's room and flung himself on her bed next to Doc.

"You guys should have waked me up. I've never seen a real fire! It must have been real exciting — all the fire engines and everything!"

Doc ruffled Teddy's mop of golden-brown curls. "Fires are never exciting, Teddy. Scary — yes. But exciting — no. Especially not in this case, when so many animals' lives were in danger."

But Teddy wasn't convinced. "I've been thinking that maybe I don't want to be an astronaut when I grow up. Maybe I want to be a fireman! I could drive one of those big fire trucks, with the sirens going 'WooooWooooWooo!' "

He reached out to grab Cleveland, but the cat slipped out of his grasp and leaped off the bed, pursued by Jocko. The two of them almost knocked Erin down as she came through the door. Erin neatly sidestepped the animals, however, and announced, "Breakfast will be ready in about ten minutes. I just put the sausages on the stove, and the pancake batter is ready whenever you are."

Erin was wearing jeans over the leotard she almost always wore, and her long blonde hair was tied back in a ponytail. Erin looked as much like Mrs.

Taylor as Val looked like Doc. Erin was fine-boned and delicate, and wanted to be a ballet dancer like her mother; Val was sturdy, tall, and dark-haired; and Teddy was a combination of both parents: solid yet slender, with bright, sparkling eyes full of mischief.

Erin joined Teddy and Doc on the edge of Val's bed. "Did I dream it, or did you and Daddy really go off to a fire in the middle of the night?" she asked Val.

"Yes, we did," Val told her. "The Humane Society shelter caught fire, and Dad and I went there to take care of the injured animals. Dad took the ones that were really hurt to Animal Inn, and I . . . well . . . I fell asleep," she admitted.

"But your big sister was a tremendous help when things were really bad," Doc said, stroking Val's tangled hair. "Honey, why don't you wash up and get dressed, and we'll all have breakfast in a few minutes?"

"That's what I was going to do," Val said. She felt a little miffed that Erin had taken over as Sunday morning breakfast-maker, but she also knew that Erin was a much better cook than she could ever be. Her sausages often turned into little charred tubes, and the pancakes were sometimes a lot browner on one side than the other. But with lots of syrup and butter, they always tasted pretty good.

"Fine," Doc said. "We all have a lot to talk about this morning. I've been on the phone with some of the other members of the Humane Society board, and we all agree that our fund-raising program must be put into high gear in order to raise enough money for a new shelter. We're going to have an old-fashioned Country Fair, and it's up to me to appoint people to handle it. You're the first person I thought of, Vallie, as chairman of my junior committee. And I thought maybe Toby might be interested in being cochairman with you."

"Hey, that's a great idea!" Val said. Toby also worked at Animal Inn, helping Doc after school and on Saturdays, and he was one of her best friends. "I bet he'd love to do it. I know I would."

"Can we be on the committee, too?" Erin asked eagerly. "Teddy and I could get lots of kids from Jackson School to help out!"

"Yeah, Vallie!" Teddy added. "Me and Billy and Eric and Sparky could make posters and stuff. And I bet Mrs. Racer would bake lots of cookies and cakes and pies to sell. We could make tons of money for the Humane Society!"

"Teddy, will you please stop bouncing?" Val begged, clutching the edge of her mattress as Teddy in his excitement used the bed as a trampoline. "You're making me seasick!"

"Yes — come on, son," said Doc, catching Teddy

in mid-bounce. "Let's leave Vallie alone so she can take her shower and get dressed. We'll talk more about the Country Fair over breakfast."

"Breakfast!" cried Erin, dashing for the door. "I forgot all about the sausages! They'll be burned to a crisp!"

"Then they'll taste just like the ones Vallie cooks," Teddy said cheerfully as Doc carried him off, with Jocko and Sunshine trotting along behind.

Val made a face at him, then bent down to peer under the bed. "It's okay, Cleveland, you can come out now," she said.

The big orange cat stalked out, looking indignant. He gave his long white whiskers a quick polish, then followed Val down the hall to the bathroom. He was fascinated by running water and loved sitting on the edge of the sink while she brushed her teeth, even though he hated getting wet.

Val showered and dressed in record time, and joined the rest of the family in the kitchen, her damp hair still wrapped in a towel.

"I'll call Toby right after breakfast," she said as Erin placed a heaping plate of pancakes in front of her on the butcher block table. (No sausages for Val — she *never* ate meat.) "I can't wait to tell him about the Fair. I wonder if he's heard about the fire last night?"

"He has if his family gets the *Essex Gazette*,"

Doc said. He showed her the front page of the paper, and Val saw a picture of herself and Doc bending over the dog with the broken leg against a background of fire engines and flames.

" 'Doctor Theodore Taylor and assistant caring for one of the residents of the Humane Society shelter during last night's fire,' " Val read aloud.

"Gee, Dad, you're famous!" Teddy said, impressed.

"I don't see why they couldn't print Vallie's name, too," said Erin.

"I don't care," Val said. " 'Assistant ' sounds much more official than 'daughter.' "

Erin craned her neck to get a closer look. "On second thought, Vallie," she said with a giggle, "maybe it's just as well they didn't give your name. Your hair's a mess!"

"Thanks a bunch," Val said sourly. "For your information, the last thing I was thinking about was how my hair looked. I didn't even know they were taking the picture; did you, Dad?"

"Nope," said Doc. "If I'd known, I would have combed my beard."

Everyone laughed at that.

"After I call Toby, can we go to Animal Inn?" Val asked when she had swallowed her last forkful of pancakes. "You don't think any of them died during the night, do you?" she asked her father anxiously.

"No, Vallie, I'm sure they haven't," Doc said. "If any of those animals had taken a turn for the worse, Mike would have been on the phone to me like a shot."

"I know. But I can't help worrying," Val said. "Can we go?"

"Of course, just as soon as the table's cleared and the dishes are in the dishwasher," Doc replied. "Teddy, you're elected to clean-up squad. Erin cooked breakfast and Vallie put in a hard night's work, so she's on vacation this morning."

"Oh, brother!" Teddy sighed. But he got up and started removing the dishes. "Can I come, too? I want to see all those cats and dogs."

Erin shuddered delicately. "*I* don't. I don't want to see them until they're all better and all their fur's grown back. Besides, I'm going over to Olivia's. We have to practice a duet for ballet class next week. And Olivia asked if I could stay for lunch. May I, Daddy?"

"Yes, Teddy, you may come with Vallie and me; and yes, Erin, you may have lunch at Olivia's. I only hope it's a *late* lunch, since it's eleven-thirty and you just finished breakfast."

"Thanks, Daddy!" Erin gave him a quick kiss

23

and ran out of the kitchen to get her toe shoes.

While Teddy was stacking the dishes in the dishwasher, Val dialed Toby's number. Someone answered after three rings.

"Toby?" Val asked after a moment's hesitation. Toby had so many brothers that she was never quite sure who she was talking to.

"No — Tom. Just a minute, I'll get Toby."

When Toby picked up, Val said, "Toby, it's Val — "

But before she could say anything more, Toby cut in. "Hey, Val, I saw the picture of you and Doc on the front page of the *Gazette*. That must've been some fire! The article said it was caused by the electrical wiring. The wires were too old, or something. You should've called me! I could've helped out."

"Everything happened too fast, Toby," Val told him. "By the time you'd have gotten there from the farm, everything would have been under control. We took the most badly injured animals to Animal Inn — we're on our way to check on them right now." No need to tell him that she'd fallen asleep on the way. Toby would just make some dumb crack and say it was "just like a girl."

"Listen, the real reason I called was that Doc wants you and me to be cochairmen of his junior committee for the Country Fair. Want to do it?"

"Whoa! Hold on. What Country Fair? What're you talking about?" Toby asked.

Val explained about the need to raise more money for a new shelter, and Toby said he thought that was a swell idea.

"Let's talk about it Tuesday at work," Val suggested. "We'll have to come up with some activities and stuff and make lots of posters."

"We can't make any posters until we know when the Fair is going to be," Toby said reasonably.

Val hadn't thought of that. "Dad, what's the date of the Country Fair?" she asked.

Doc shrugged. "You got me. Since we only decided on it this morning, none of the details are firmed up. But we're talking about early June. I'll have more information after the next Humane Society board meeting."

"I heard," Toby said when Val began to repeat what Doc had said. "We don't have to worry about posters for a while yet, anyway. You said you're going to Animal Inn right now?"

"In a couple of minutes," Val said.

"I'll bike over and meet you there. We can start making plans right away. Hey, Val, you know what? I just got a great idea! I bet I could talk my dad into contributing ice cream to sell at the Fair — maybe we could have an ice cream-eating contest, too!"

"That *is* a great idea," Val agreed. Curran's Dairy made the best ice cream she'd ever tasted. "Okay. See you in a little while."

"What's a great idea?" Teddy asked as she hung up the phone.

"An ice cream-eating contest. Toby thinks Mr. Curran would donate lots of ice cream for the Country Fair."

"Wow!" Teddy's eyes lit up. "I'm going to enter! And I bet I win, too. I can eat more ice cream than anybody in the whole third grade!"

"And you could most likely get sicker than anybody in the whole third grade, too," Doc said. "But it's a little early to think about that now. You ready, Val, Teddy?"

"I'm ready but Vallie's not," Teddy said.

"Yes, I am." Val started for the door. "Come on, let's go."

"Not just yet, Vallie," said Doc. "Not unless you're in disguise as an Indian rajah."

Val looked at him blankly. "Huh?"

Doc patted her towel-wrapped head. "Better finish drying your hair first, honey."

"Oh, gosh! I completely forgot." Val took off the towel. Her hair was almost dry, but she knew Doc wouldn't let her go out of the house with it still damp, even though it wasn't very cold this morning.

"It'll only take a second to blow it dry," she said, and ran upstairs.

"Girls!" Teddy said disgustedly. "I'm glad I don't have to mess with all that hair."

"So am I," Doc agreed. "You'd look pretty silly if your hair was as long as Vallie's or Erin's. Come on, son," Doc teased. "Us men will go wait in the van."

Chapter
3

The minute the vet van pulled up in front of Animal Inn, Val and Teddy leaped out. The first thing they saw was a cardboard carton sitting on the steps in front of the main entrance to the clinic. Val reached the box first and looked inside. Four pairs of bright yellow eyes looked back at her, and four small pink mouths opened and began to mew.

Val reached in and patted each kitten in turn. At first she'd thought that Miss Maggie had had a change of heart and had dumped Calico's babies, but she immediately realized that these kittens were bigger and older.

"Aren't they adorable?" she crooned, picking up a fluffy little striped ball of fur and cuddling it under her chin. "But what are they doing here?"

"Boy, Vallie, your head really isn't on straight today," Teddy said. "Did you forget how to read?" He shoved a piece of paper under her nose. "This was taped to the front of the box. It says, 'Sorry the animal shelter burned down. Saw the article in the paper this morning and figured I better bring the kittens here. We got too many cats.' It's signed, 'An animal-lover.' "

"Uh-oh!" Val looked up at her father, who had just joined them. "Dad, it looks like people think we're taking over for the shelter."

"And them kittens isn't the first, not by a long shot!" said Mike Strickler, opening the door to Animal Inn's waiting room. It was the very first time Val had ever seen Mike look upset. No matter what happened, Mike always looked like a cheerful old leprechaun. Nothing had ever fazed Mike . . . until now.

"You mean other people have brought their unwanted pets to Animal Inn?" Doc asked.

"You bet I do," Mike said. "We got a German shepherd and two funny-lookin' pups so far. Don't know where we're gonna put 'em. We're full up with the animals that were hurt in the fire."

Teddy carried the carton containing the three remaining kittens into the waiting room and put it on the floor. Val carefully put the one she was holding back with its brothers and sisters.

"But why — " Doc began, but Mike cut him off.

"It was that article in this morning's paper. Seems like everybody in Essex read it."

"What did the article say, anyway?" Val asked.

"We only read the caption under the picture of Dad and me."

"It said that you was takin' the animals that was hurt to Animal Inn. That's all, but people seem to think that this is the new animal shelter. You're gonna have to order some more pet food, Doc," Mike said. "We're runnin' low, and if we get any more boarders, we're gonna be fresh out." He looked down at the carton full of kittens at his feet. "Don't know where we're gonna put those little guys. Don't hardly have any space at all."

Teddy was kneeling by the box, and the kittens were tumbling all over themselves, playing with his fingers.

"Dad, maybe we could. . . ."

"Yes, Dad! Just for a little while," Val put in.

"Ye gods!" Doc groaned. "We have a cat, two dogs, four rabbits, four hamsters, a duck, and Teddy's chickens, and you're asking me to take in four kittens?"

"Not forever," Val said quickly. "Just until we can find someone to adopt them. And they're so cute and cuddly, I bet we'll find homes for them real fast."

Doc rubbed his beard the way he always did when he was faced with a problem. "I'll think about it," he said at last, and Val and Teddy looked at each other, smiling triumphantly. When Doc said he'd think about it, he almost always ended up saying yes.

Doc caught the look. "I said I'd *think* about it," he said firmly. "Now let's take a look at our patients. How are they doing, Mike?"

"Oh, they're shaping up real good," Mike said. "Five cats and four dogs, and every one of 'em yellin' for their breakfast first thing this morning. I been checking on 'em every few hours just in case somebody had a relapse or something, but even that dog with the busted leg and the hair burned off his rear end looks right perky."

"Oh, good!" Val said happily. "Let's go take a look at them."

"Hey, Val!" Toby burst in the door and almost tripped over the box of kittens. But he sidestepped at the last minute, and went on, "Guess what! I talked to my dad, and he says he'll be glad to donate ice cream to the Fair and sponsor the contest. Isn't that cool? Hi, Doc. How you doing, Teddy? How're the new patients, Mike?" Before anyone could respond, he glanced down at the kittens, really seeing them for the first time. "What's the matter with these fellas?" he asked. "They don't look injured or burned to me."

"They're not," Teddy said. "They're orphans. Somebody left them here 'cause there's no animal shelter anymore. We're gonna take them home with us — " He looked quickly at Doc. "Maybe."

"Unless you could use a few cats at the farm,"

Doc added hopefully. "It looks to me as though they'll grow up to be terrific mousers."

"Gee, Doc," Toby said, "I'd really like to take them, but we have so many cats now that there aren't enough mice to go around."

"How about dogs?" Mike asked. "We got a German shepherd and a couple of mongrel pups inside, too. Don't know what we're gonna do with 'em."

"Pups?" Toby looked interested. "Somebody dump them, too?"

"That's right," Val said. "People seem to think Animal Inn's taking over where the shelter left off."

Just then the phone rang. Val went to the reception desk and picked up the receiver. "Animal Inn, good morning," she said in her "professional" voice. " . . . A pet raccoon? What's wrong with him? . . . Oh, I see. . . . No, I'm sorry. We can't take any more animals unless they're really sick. . . . No, the only ones we took from the shelter were the ones that got hurt in the fire. . . . I'm sorry, I really am. Why don't you take him out into the country and let him loose? Wild animals ought to go back to their natural habitat. . . . You're welcome. 'Bye."

Val hung up. "That was another one," she said. "Dad, I think we ought to call the *Gazette* and ask them to print a notice saying that Animal Inn is *not* the new animal shelter!"

"Exactly what I was thinking," Doc said. "I'll

32

call first thing tomorrow morning. Nobody will be there at this hour on a Sunday."

"Mike, can I see those pups now?" Toby asked eagerly.

"You sure can," Mike said. "I put 'em in the Large Animal Clinic, in one of the stalls. Nowhere else for 'em to go."

He and Toby headed for the barn that served as Animal Inn's Large Animal Clinic, and Doc, Teddy, and Val went into the infirmary where the injured animals had been placed in cages. They were greeted by loud barking and shrill meows. Val was glad to see that all the patients were on their feet, furry faces pressed up against the wire mesh. As she went from cage to cage, talking softly to each animal, Doc examined them briefly.

"Wow! Look at that cat!" Teddy said, peering into one cage. "I never saw a cat with its whiskers burned off before. And it's *bald*, too!"

"The fur will grow back, Teddy, and so will the whiskers," Doc assured him. "He'll be ready to go home in a few days — if he has a home to go to."

"I wonder if Miss Maggie could take in a few more pets," Val mused, patting a shaggy little mongrel with two bandaged front paws.

"Afraid not, Vallie," Doc said. "Miss Maggie's done more than her share. We mustn't impose on her good nature."

33

"Miss Maggie?" Teddy echoed. "You mean that crazy old lady who rides her bicycle all over town like the Wicked Witch of the West in *The Wizard of Oz?*"

"Miss Maggie is *not* a crazy old lady," Doc said sternly. "She's a fine person and she loves animals. She took home a lot of dogs and cats last night, and she'll give them excellent care. Don't make fun of her, Teddy."

"I'm sorry," Teddy said, hanging his head. "I wasn't making fun of her, not really. It's just that she looks kinda . . . *strange*. And a lot of the kids *say* she's a witch," he added defiantly.

"Teddy, that's the dopiest thing I ever heard!" Val said. "You know there isn't any such thing as a witch. And if there was, Miss Maggie wouldn't be one. Like Dad says, she has a heart of gold."

Teddy's eyes lit up. "*Real* gold? Boy, she must be worth a lot of money!" Val scowled at him, and he said quickly, "Just kidding, Vallie. I know that's just a 'spression."

"An *expression*, Teddy," Doc corrected. "Now if you will kindly move away from this poor bald, whiskerless creature, I'd like to check him out."

Satisfied that all the animals were doing well, Val decided to go into the barn and see the new boarders. Then she'd saddle up The Ghost and go for a ride before she let him out into the pasture.

She found Toby in the stall next to The Ghost, rolling in the clean, sweet-smelling straw with two roly-poly puppies. They were jumping all over him, licking his face and chewing on his jeans, his shoes, and anything else they could sink their little sharp teeth into. The German shepherd was looking on, like an indulgent parent watching his children at play. As for The Ghost, he had stretched his neck as far as he could into the adjoining stall, flicking his ears back and forth. He wasn't used to so much activity next door, and it was obvious to Val that he didn't quite know what to make of it.

When The Ghost saw Val, he came to the front of his stall and whickered softly as she put her arms around his neck and rested her cheek against him.

"Looks like that horse is kinda jealous of them babies," Mike said. He'd been checking on some of the other animals in the Large Animal Clinic, and now he came over to The Ghost's stall. He pulled a fat carrot from the hip pocket of his faded overalls and offered it to the horse. The Ghost lifted the carrot from Mike's outstretched palm with velvety lips and crunched it contentedly between his big yellow teeth.

"There's nothing to be jealous of, Ghost," Val said, stroking his satiny neck. "Those poor little puppies are only here because they don't have anywhere else to go. But you belong here. You're my horse and I love you a lot. Toby loves you, too, you know.

35

But those little puppies are awful cute. And maybe, just maybe, Toby's folks will let him adopt them or one of them, anyway."

"What about that German shepherd? That's what I'd like to know," Mike said. "He ain't young and cute — his muzzle's all gray — but he's a good dog, all right. What's gonna happen to him?"

"I don't know, Mike," Val said, looking over at the big dog. "I wonder why his owners gave him up?"

Mike shook his head. "Dunno." He gazed at the German shepherd and smiled a little. "I call him Ludwig. Dunno what his real name is, but Ludwig seems to suit him somehow."

"Like Beethoven," Val said.

"Well, I don't care about no German composer, but I used to know a fella name of Ludwig Heinz. Owned the feed store some years ago. He looked kinda like a dog."

Val snorted with laughter. "You know *everybody*, don't you, Mike?" she said.

"Everybody who's ever lived around Essex," Mike said. "What's so funny?"

"Nothing," Val said hastily. Suddenly she had a thought. "Mike, you don't have any pets, do you?"

"Nah," Mike said. "What do I need pets for? I got all these animals to take care of. Have some real good conversations with 'em, too. Don't need any pets."

"But when you go home after you're through at Animal Inn, don't you get . . . lonely?" Val asked.

"Lonely? Me?" Mike looked astonished. "Never been lonely in my life, and I been alive for about a century, give or take a year or two."

Val giggled. "Oh, Mike! You can't be as old as all that! I bet you're not as old as Miss Maggie Rafferty."

"That's for me to know and you to find out," Mike said, and Val sighed. She'd been trying for years to learn Mike's age, but he always managed to avoid telling her.

Suddenly Mike's twinkling blue eyes narrowed. "All this talk about me being lonely . . . you're not suggestin' I should hitch up with Miss Maggie, are you, Vallie?" he asked suspiciously. " 'Cause if you are, you can just forget it! I was born a bachelor and I'll die a bachelor. Don't need no cranky old woman meddling in my life, nosirree!"

The thought had never entered Val's head. "Oh, no, Mike," she assured him. "I wasn't thinking about Miss Maggie. But I *was* thinking about Ludwig. He needs a home and he likes you, I can tell. Look at the way he's wagging his tail."

Mike looked. "That ain't the worst idea in the

world. Rather live with a dog than a woman any day of the week." He leaned over and scratched Ludwig's head. "I'll think about it. I'm not makin' no promises, but I'll think about it."

Val beamed. "You do that, Mike!"

"Val, come take a look at these pups," Toby said. Wisps of straw were sticking out of his curly brown hair, and his face was flushed with pleasure. "The fat one with the curly tail really likes me, I can tell. And the one that's not so fat likes me, too. I'm going to ask my folks if I can adopt them. We only have one dog at the farm. I bet they'd say yes!"

Val entered the stall and knelt down beside Toby. The pups immediately started yapping happily and jumping all over her. She giggled as two wet pink tongues licked her face.

"That would be wonderful, Toby," she said. "I wonder what kind of dog they are? Or I guess I should say, what kind of *dogs*. They're a mixed breed all right, but it's hard to tell what they're going to look like when they're so little and chubby."

"I don't care," Toby said cheerfully. "But I bet they grow up to be pretty big. Look at those paws! They're huge. Looks like they're wearing boxing gloves."

The Ghost tossed his head and snorted in disgust at all the attention the puppies were receiving.

"I'll be with you in a minute, Ghost," Val said,

rolling the fatter pup onto his back and rubbing his round little stomach. "Then we'll go for a ride."

"Vallie? Where are you?" Teddy came running into the barn.

"Over here, Teddy. Come see the pups," Val called.

He entered the stall, saying, "Guess what, Vallie! Miss Maggie Rafferty just called, and I answered the phone just the way you do. I said, 'Good morning, Animal Inn,' and she said. . . ." He saw the pups, and flung himself onto the straw between Toby and Val. "Oh, boy, are they ever cute! Hey, Vallie, do you think Dad would let us take them home? I bet Jocko and Sunshine would like having puppies to play with!"

"But Cleveland wouldn't," Val said. "Besides, Toby's going to ask his parents if he can adopt them. There's lots of room at the Currans' farm for puppies to run and play."

"Oh." Teddy's face fell, but only for a moment. "Hey, Toby, if you *do* adopt them, can I come and play with them? What're you gonna name them? Are they boys or girls?"

"Sure, you can play with them," Toby said. "I haven't decided what I'll call them yet. The fat one's a boy and the other one's a girl. Watch out, they have real sharp little teeth."

The German shepherd came over to Teddy and

Teddy patted him. "Is he their father?" Teddy asked Val.

"I don't think so," Val said. "His name is Ludwig, or at least, that's what Mike calls him. Maybe Mike's going to adopt him."

"Now, Vallie, I told you I'd think about it," Mike said. "Haven't made up my mind yet. I'm still thinkin'."

Teddy was rolling around in the straw with the puppies, giggling and squealing as they pounced on him with high-pitched yips. They were making so much noise that Val didn't hear her father calling her until he stood by the stall door.

"Vallie, are you coming with me?" he asked.

Val looked up, startled. "Coming with you? Where?" she asked.

"Out to John Wetzel's farm. Didn't Teddy give you the message?"

Teddy sat up, clutching a puppy in his arms. "Gee, Dad, I kinda forgot. I'm sorry."

"I can see you've had some powerful distractions," Doc said with a smile. "Vallie, Miss Maggie phoned to say that she's just learned from a 'reliable source' that John Wetzel recently acquired a burro, and he's been mistreating it. From what Miss Maggie says, he's beaten the poor animal almost to death. She may be exaggerating, but knowing Miss Maggie, I'm inclined to believe she has all the facts. I told her I'd go out there right away and look into it. I may need help. Do you want to come with me?"

Val jumped to her feet. "Oh, yes, Dad! I'll get your bag." She was about to run off, when she remembered The Ghost. Flinging her arms around the horse's neck, she said, "Sorry about our ride, Ghost, but I'll be back later."

"I'll let him out into the pasture, Vallie," Mike said. "You run along now."

Toby stood up, too, brushing the straw off his clothes. "Can I come, Doc? I don't know Mr. Wetzel, but I've heard my dad talk about him. He says he's really mean. If he gets nasty, you might need another man to back you up."

"I doubt if it will come to that, Toby," Doc said, "but you're welcome to come along."

"I'll stay here and keep the puppies company," Teddy said. "I don't want them to get lonely."

Doc smiled. "You do that, Teddy. Vallie, bring my bag. Toby and I will meet you in the van."

Val hurried into the Small Animal Clinic, anger building inside her. How could anybody abuse an animal? Toby must be right — Mr. Wetzel must be a very mean man!

Chapter
4

"What a grungy-looking farm!" Val said as Doc drove the vet van down a bumpy dirt road toward a cluster of dilapidated buildings. The barn badly needed a coat of paint, and the roof sagged in the middle like a swaybacked horse. A few ramshackle chicken coops huddled nearby, with some scrawny chickens pecking at the ground and each other. A sow and her piglets wallowed in the muddy yard of the pig sty. Val held her nose.

"Whew! What a smell!" she gasped.

The farmhouse was in the same condition as the rest of the buildings: weathered, sagging, and covered with blistering paint that might once have been white. A vicious-looking dog was tied by a rope to the front porch, barking frantically. It seemed as if he couldn't wait to tear the unwelcome visitors limb from limb.

"My dad says Mr. Wetzel's the kind of man who gives farmers a bad name," Toby said. "He says it's no disgrace to be poor, but it *is* a disgrace to be poor, mean, and dirty."

Doc slowed the van to a stop next to the barnyard. The smell from the manure pile combined with the pig sty made Val feel as though she was going to be sick.

"You and Toby stay here," Doc said, getting out of the van. "I'll see if I can find Mr. Wetzel."

He didn't have far to look. A leathery man in filthy overalls came out of the barn, carrying a pitchfork. The man was wearing a battered straw hat, and the eyes that peered from beneath the brim were small and close-set. He reminded Val of the pet ferret Teddy had once had — only Frank the ferret had been very friendly — and this man definitely was not.

"What you doing on my property?" he shouted at Doc. "Didn't you see the sign down by the road? 'No trespassing,' it says. Can't you read?"

Doc kept his voice very calm. "I'm Doctor Theodore Taylor. Are you John Wetzel?"

"So what if I am? What you doing here? Ain't nobody sick. Don't need no doctor."

"What did I tell you?" Toby said to Val. "Mean, that's what he is."

"I'm a veterinarian," Doc said. "I'm also a member of the Essex Humane Society. It's been reported that you are the owner of a burro named Pedro. Is that correct?"

"None of your business if it is," Mr. Wetzel growled. "What're you snooping around here for, anyways? My animals is my business."

"It's Humane Society business when we learn of an animal that is being mistreated," Doc told him. His voice was steely now, and he looked Wetzel straight in his shifty little eyes.

Wetzel tightened his grip on the pitchfork, and Val clutched Toby's arm. What if he stabbed her father with those sharp tines? Toby flung open the door of the van and jumped out, followed by Val. They ran to Doc's side.

"Who says?" Wetzel blustered. "Who says I been mistreating Pedro?"

"Then you *do* have a burro named Pedro," Doc said.

Wetzel scowled. "What if I do? Ain't no business of yours *or* the Humane Society, whatever that is." He glared at Val and Toby. "Who're them kids? You're trespassing, all three of you. I'll call the police on you, that's what I'll do!"

"I don't think so, Mr. Wetzel," Doc said quietly. "Because if you do, and if you have indeed mistreated the burro, you'll be served with a summons for animal abuse. As for these young people here, they are my daughter Valentine, and my assistant, Toby Curran."

"Curran, huh?" Wetzel's scowl was now focused on Toby. "Your dad's the big-shot dairy farmer, right? You ain't got no right poking your nose in where it don't belong."

Toby's ears turned bright red, and he clenched his fists at his sides. But before he could speak, Doc said, "Why don't you let me take a look at the burro, Mr. Wetzel? If he's in good health, there's no problem. If he's unwell, I can help him. I strongly advise you to cooperate with me, Mr. Wetzel. Believe me, you won't benefit from a full-scale investigation of your farm by the Humane Society."

Suddenly Mr. Wetzel seemed to collapse, to deflate, as though he were a balloon somebody had let the air out of. His voice shriveled into a whine.

"Well, Doc, it's like this. I'm a poor man — you can see that. I ain't got no fancy machinery to help me work my land. Can't hardly make ends meet, the economy being what it is. So when I heard that the U.S. Bureau of Land Management was offering these burros up for adoption, I figured I could use a free animal. Them burros is strong as horses, maybe stronger, even though they're small. I figured I could get me a free burro and break him, see — they're wild when they round 'em up out west — and teach him to haul and plow.

"But *this* burro's something else! No matter how hard I tried, I couldn't get him to pull a plow. I got a bad one, Doc. There's good animals and there's

45

bad animals, and Pedro's a bad animal, that's for certain sure! He ain't done nothing but eat his fool head off and kick and bite since the day I got him. So every now and then I hit him, you know what I mean?

"It's like with kids. . . ." He cast a vicious glance at Toby and Val. "Spare the rod and spoil the child, right, Doc? Well, that goes double with donkeys! Ain't nothing stubborner than a donkey, unless it's a mule, and I ain't had no experience with mules. So as far as I'm concerned, donkeys is the stubbornest there is. You keep that in mind, Doc, when you take a look at this here animal of mine. And remember, I given him a good home when he was down and out, and he never appreciated it, not one bit!"

A good home! Val thought, biting her lip to keep from telling Mr. Wetzel exactly what she thought of his "good home."

"May I see Pedro now?" Doc asked. Only the whiteness of his knuckles as he held onto the handle of his bag showed how angry he was.

"Sure. But remember what I told you. He's a bad animal, Doc. That's why I had to hit him sometimes."

Wetzel led the way through the smelly barnyard with Doc, Val, and Toby at his heels. They entered the dilapidated barn, and Wetzel stopped in front of a stall filled with dirty straw.

It was so dark that Val could hardly see the burro standing in the shadows. But when her eyes became accustomed to the gloom, she saw a little donkey standing, head hanging. Flies buzzed around him, lighting on the oozing welts on his back.

"There he is," Wetzel said. "Stubborn, that's what he is. Tried to teach him who's boss, but he wouldn't listen."

At the sound of Wetzel's voice, the burro, weak as he was, laid his long furry ears back and lashed out with his two hind hooves.

"See what I mean?" Wetzel said triumphantly.

"Yes, I see," Doc said. "Indeed, I do."

It was all Val could do to keep herself from bursting into tears. She had never seen an animal in such bad shape — unless it was Gigi the monkey and Leo the lion cub from Mr. Zefferelli's menagerie at the carnival last fall. Pedro was obviously on his last legs, but he hadn't given up. He'd fight till his last breath against the man who had beaten him so badly. And it looked as if his last breath wasn't very far away.

Doc didn't even bother to examine the burro — he didn't need to.

"This animal is going to die unless we get him to Animal Inn right away," he said grimly. "He's too big to fit into the van." He turned to Wetzel. "Do you have a truck?"

"What if I do?" Wetzel shifted his feet uneasily in the filthy straw, avoiding Doc's eyes.

"Get it!" Doc commanded between clenched teeth. Val had never seen her father so furious.

"Now hold on there just one minute," Wetzel blustered. "What you want my truck for?"

"We are going to put this burro into your truck, and you are going to drive it to Animal Inn," Doc said. "I am going to try to save Pedro's life. I can't treat him here; I need all the resources my veterinary clinic can provide."

"Well, now, I don't know . . ." Wetzel began, but Doc cut him off.

"Wetzel, *get that truck!*"

The farmer stared at him, then glanced from Val to Toby. The expressions he saw on all three faces seemed to convince him, because he turned and shuffled out of the stall, mumbling under his breath.

When he was no longer in sight, Val cried, "Dad, that man ought to be put in jail! He's almost *killed* that poor burro!"

"I wish we could give him a taste of his own medicine," Toby said. "I'd like to beat him the way he beat Pedro!"

"So would I," Doc said grimly. "But we mustn't lose sight of the most important thing, and that's Pedro's health. I'll see that Wetzel receives a summons for animal cruelty. He'll have to pay a heavy

48

fine, or risk a jail sentence. I only hope we're not too late to save Pedro's life."

Val moved closer to the burro, but Pedro managed to raise his drooping head and tried to bite her outstretched hand.

"I'm not going to hurt you," she whispered. "We want to *help* you! We're not like that terrible man. Don't be afraid."

"Keep away, Vallie," Doc said, drawing her close to his side. "He's never known kindness, so he doesn't know how to respond. If he lives, perhaps we can teach him to trust human beings. Up to now, he's only known cruelty and abuse."

Val stood next to Doc, his arm around her shoulders, gazing sadly at the burro. *Were* they too late? What if Pedro died right then and there? He was weaving on his feet, breathing in deep, raspy gasps.

"Oh, Dad!" she cried, burying her face in his chest.

A clanking, rattling noise filled the barn as an ancient pickup truck backed in, spewing clouds of exhaust smoke that made Val choke.

"Come on, Toby. Help me get Pedro into the truck," Doc said. He went to the burro's head and grasped the frayed halter. Pedro made an effort to bite and kick, but he was too weak. As Doc pulled gently on the halter, the burro staggered after him. He didn't resist when Doc and Toby lifted him into the bed of the pickup. He was so thin that he didn't weigh much at all.

Wetzel stuck his head out of the cab. "I want you to know, Doc, that you're taking my property!" he yelled. "Stealing, that's what it is. Stealing my truck, too, if it comes to that!"

Doc went over to him. "And I want *you* to know, Wetzel, that if this animal dies, you are going to be in very big trouble. As it is, you'll receive a summons first thing tomorrow morning. I strongly suggest that you pay the fine and mend your ways, or you'll find yourself in jail and your farm, such as it is, on the auction block!" He glanced at Val and Toby. "Come on, kids. Get into the van. We'll lead the way to Animal Inn. Follow me," he told Wetzel.

A moment later, the vet van was jouncing down the bumpy dirt road, Wetzel's pickup close behind.

"It'll be a miracle if Pedro survives the trip," Toby muttered, and Val agreed. She could only hope that the feisty little burro had enough strength left in him to make it to the clinic. Nobody else said a word for the rest of the drive. All three were lost in their own thoughts, and each knew exactly what the other was thinking, so there was no need for speech.

Doc turned down Orchard Lane at last. The trip had seemed endless to Val. She craned her neck to make sure that Wetzel was still following. She wouldn't have put it past him to give them the slip, continuing down the York Road. But he didn't. Doc drove around to the entrance of the Large Animal Clinic and stopped the van. Val and Toby leaped out.

"I'll tell Mike to give us a hand with Pedro," Toby said, running into the barn. He almost bumped into Teddy, who was coming out at the same time.

"Where's the burro?" Teddy asked. "Is he in that crummy truck?"

"Yes, he is," Val said.

"Where are we going to put him? There aren't any empty stalls." Teddy trotted along beside Val as she joined Doc at the rear of the pickup.

Val hadn't thought of that, but Doc had.

"Teddy, you can be a big help," he said. "Take those puppies into the examining room — the German shepherd, too. We'll use that stall for the burro. Run along, now," he added, since Teddy didn't seem to be in any hurry to do as he was told.

"Can't I see the burro?" Teddy asked. "I've never seen a real burro up close."

Val knew that Doc didn't want Teddy to see Pedro in his present condition, so she said, "You'll see him in a little while, Teddy. Do what Dad says. And stay with the dogs until they get accustomed to the examining room. And you'd better check on those kittens, too. I bet they're lonely and scared."

Teddy brightened. "Oh, yeah! I forgot about the kittens. I'll be right back!"

51

He ran off as Toby and Mike came out of the barn. Wetzel just sat in the cab of the truck, scowling and muttering to himself.

Very carefully, Doc, Toby, and Mike lifted the burro from the bed of the truck and carried him into the barn while Val watched anxiously. Wetzel revved the rackety engine and began backing down the drive. Right before he turned onto Orchard Lane, he stuck his head out the window and hollered, "Stealing, that's what it is! I'll have the law on you, just see if I don't!" Then the pickup lurched down the road, trailing clouds of black smoke.

Fists clenched, Val shouted after him, "Pedro's not a bad animal! *You're* a bad man! I hope when you get home, your horrible dog eats you for dinner!" She knew he couldn't hear her, but it made her feel a little better. Then she went into the barn to find out what she could do to help her father.

Chapter
5

Doc injected Pedro with painkiller and a sedative so he and Val could tend to the burro's welts and bruises without being bitten or kicked. He also gave him a shot of antibiotic to prevent infection from the many open sores on Pedro's body. Val mixed up a bucket of warm mash, which Pedro sniffed at suspiciously but did not eat. Mike promised he'd talk the burro into sampling it later on, after everyone had left.

"He don't trust nobody," Mike said, shaking his head sadly, "and I can't hardly blame him. You just leave me alone with him for a while and we'll have a nice long talk, just the two of us, in peace and quiet."

Val sighed. "I guess he hasn't had much of that, poor thing."

"We've done all we can for now, Vallie," Doc said. "It'll take some time, but Pedro will recover." He looked around. "Where's Toby? He was here just a minute ago."

"I think he went to call his parents about the puppies," Val told him. "And I guess Teddy's still playing with the kittens."

Doc groaned. "The kittens! They completely slipped my mind."

"You said we could keep them for a little while, until we find homes for them," Val reminded him, and Doc nodded.

"So I did. I should have my head examined. Better collect them and Teddy, and we'll be on our way. I don't know about you, but my stomach barely remembers those pancakes and sausages. It's crying out for lunch. . . ." He checked his watch. "And no wonder, it's a quarter after three."

Val realized that her stomach was grumbling, too, and then she remembered The Ghost. She'd been looking forward to a ride this afternoon, but there wouldn't be enough time.

"I'll be back in a minute, Dad," she said, and ran out of the barn to the pasture where the big dapple gray horse was contentedly grazing. He raised his head at her whistle and trotted over to the fence.

"Sorry, Ghost," she said, rubbing behind his ears. "We'll have to have our ride tomorrow after school, okay?"

The Ghost nodded his head as though he understood.

"When Mike takes you back to your stall, you're

54 as just number

54

going to have a surprise," Val continued. "There's a burro in the stall next to yours. He's not very friendly, but that's because nobody's ever been kind to him. The man who owned him beat him something awful. You be nice to him, Ghost," she said. "I bet horses and burros speak the same language. Between you and Mike, you'll probably have him feeling right at home in no time."

She gave the horse a kiss on his velvety nose, then hurried back to the clinic. Toby met her in the doorway, a broad grin on his face.

"My mom and dad say it's okay for me to bring the puppies home!" he told her.

"Oh, Toby, that's wonderful!" Val cried. "But you can't take them with you on your bike. We'll give you a lift in the van. I'm sure Dad won't mind."

Doc was more than happy to transport Toby and the pups, so Toby lifted his bike into the back of the van and then climbed in himself, one squirming puppy under each arm. Teddy joined him, carrying the box of squeaking kittens. The minute he put the box down, the kittens started trying to climb out. The puppies came over to investigate, and the kittens all arched their backs and fluffed up their tails, hissing and spitting like Halloween cats. To keep the peace, Val took the box of kittens into the front seat, leaving Teddy to play happily with the pups.

Doc was just starting the engine, when Val said, "Oh, dear, what about Ludwig?"

Her father gave her a weary look. "Who or what is Ludwig?" he asked.

"The German shepherd, Dad. I tried to talk Mike into adopting him, but he didn't promise. Until he makes up his mind, maybe we could. . . ."

"No," Doc said, and his tone of voice left no room for argument. "Not one more animal. Not even a field mouse, let alone a German shepherd." He glanced out the window. "Is *that* Ludwig?"

Val looked, too. She saw Mike standing in the doorway of the Small Animal Clinic with Ludwig slowly and contentedly wagging his tail beside him.

"That's Ludwig, all right," Val said, "and it looks like he's found his master."

"Ain't making no promises, Vallie," Mike called. "Don't need some big old dog messin' up my life." But as he spoke, he was patting Ludwig's head.

"They make a nice couple," Doc said with a grin, and headed the vet van down Orchard Lane.

It was only after they had dropped Toby and the pups at the Currans' farm that Val realized that she hadn't talked to him at all about the Humane Society Country Fair. There had just been too many other things going on. But they'd get together on Tuesday, when they both would be working at Animal Inn.

In the meantime, Val would start organizing her

committee. Teddy and Erin were already lined up, and that meant they'd involve their friends at Jackson School. Right after lunch, Val decided she'd call her best friend, Jill Dearborne. Jill would have lots of good ideas about how to make money; she was always on fund-raising committees at Alexander Hamilton Junior High. And besides, Val thought, firmly replacing an escaping kitten into the carton with the others, I bet she'd just love an adorable, fuzzy little pet!

Jill came right over to the Taylors' after Val — between bites of a peanut-butter-and-jelly sandwich — called her on the phone.

"Come see the kittens, Jill," Erin said the minute Jill walked in the door. "They're just the cutest things you ever saw!" Erin had come home with her friend Olivia, and both girls were sitting on the living room floor, letting the kittens climb all over them.

"They're up for grabs, Jill," Val said, scooping up the calico one and handing it to her friend. "This one's a girl. All calicos are female, isn't that interesting?"

"Oh, I *love* her!" Jill cooed. "How could anybody bear to give away anything so little and helpless?" The kitten sank its tiny sharp claws into her arm, and Jill made a face, adding, "Well, maybe not helpless, but little, anyway." She perched the kitten on her shoulder, holding it next to her cheek with one hand. "I wonder how Mom would feel about adding another member to the family?"

"I bet she'd like it," Val said enthusiastically. "Cats aren't any trouble at all, and they're very clean, too." Jill's mother was an interior decorator, and the Dearbornes' house was picture perfect. It always looked as though it was ready for a photographer to take pictures for *House and Garden*. Jill was an only child, so there was none of the comfortable clutter that was typical of the Taylors'.

"I don't know," Jill said, cuddling the kitten. "They shed, and sometimes they claw the furniture. That's why we had to give my other cat away — he ripped up Mom's favorite chair. Maybe if we had it declawed. . . ."

Val suppressed a shudder. She hated it when people brought their cats in to have their claws removed. How could a cat defend itself or climb trees without any claws? But she said, "Why don't you talk it over with your mother? You could even take the kitten home with you, to show her how cute it is."

"Maybe I will," Jill mused. "I think I'll call her Patches. . . . Speaking of cats, where's Cleveland?"

"Sulking," Val said. "He took one look at the kittens, hissed, and shot upstairs to my room. He's been under the bed ever since. Teddy took the dogs out back. They think the kittens are brand-new furry toys. They wouldn't *mean* to hurt them, but I'm afraid they'll play too rough."

Jill plopped down on the sofa, Patches still on her shoulder. "Let's talk about this Country Fair. I think it sounds like a lot of fun, and the Humane Society sure could use the money. What can I do to help?"

"You can give me some ideas about activities for kids," Val said, sitting down beside her. "And if there's anybody you can think of who might be willing to donate raffle prizes or stuff for sale — friends of your parents, maybe — see if you can get them interested. But the main job of my committee is to come up with things for kids to do. We can't charge much money, but that's okay because kids will come with their parents, and that's where the profit comes in."

The two girls put their heads together, and with suggestions from Erin and Olivia, they came up with a list of possible activities for the Country Fair. Jill volunteered to do clown makeup on the little children, and Erin said she'd help. Olivia thought a three-legged race would be fun. Val decided on a pet show, with prizes for Fattest Cat, Smallest Pet, Most Unusual Pet, and other categories that she'd think of later. When Teddy came in from playing with the dogs, he said that his cub scout troop would probably like to help out. He thought there should be a parade, and the cubs would march in it.

"A parade!" Val cried. "That's a great idea, Teddy. Let's ask Dad about it right away! Everybody in town would turn out for a parade, and we could lead them straight to the Fair."

"Where's the Fair going to be?" Jill asked.

"We'll ask Dad that, too," Val said.

"Ask Dad what?"

Doc had just come into the living room. He picked up a kitten that was skittering past his feet and gave it to Teddy. He smiled at Jill, who was sitting with Patches curled up in a little calico ball in her lap, sound asleep. "I see you've found a friend, Jill."

"Her name's Patches," Jill told him. "Or it will be, if Mom lets me keep her. We've been talking about the Country Fair. I'm going to help and I'm sure lots of our friends at school will, too."

"Dad, where's the Fair going to be held?" Val asked. "And can we have a parade? Teddy's cub scout troop will march, and the Humane Society could have a float, and maybe I could ride The Ghost!"

"A parade's a great idea," Doc agreed. "As for the site of the Fair, I just finished talking to Miss Maggie Rafferty on the phone, and she's willing to let us use the grounds of the old Rafferty mansion.

It's not too far from the center of town, and there's plenty of room."

"Did you tell her about Pedro?" Val asked.

"Who's Pedro?" asked Jill.

So Doc told Jill, Erin, and Olivia all about the burro. "As I told Miss Maggie, I've called Sheriff Weigel," Doc said, "and someone will be at Mr. Wetzel's farm first thing tomorrow morning with a summons."

"It's bad enough, abandoning poor little innocent kittens," Jill said, stroking Patches, "but it's even *worse* when somebody hurts an animal the way that man hurt Pedro! What'll happen to Pedro, Doc? Are you going to keep him at Animal Inn?"

"Yeah, Dad, are we?" Teddy asked eagerly. "When he gets better, we can train him, and then I could ride him! I bet he's just the right size for me."

"We'll keep him until he's completely healed," Doc said, "and then we'll try to find him a home. If all else fails, Wildlife Farm might take him in. But we are *not* going to add Pedro to the Taylor menagerie, Teddy, so don't get your hopes up."

"Just thought I'd ask," Teddy said. "I haven't even seen him yet. When *can* I see him, Dad?"

"I want to see him, too," Erin said. "But not until he's much better. I don't like to look at animals when they're sick or injured."

61

"You can both see him soon," Doc said. "Now let's get back to the Country Fair. Suppose you all tell me what you've cooked up so far."

Erin, Teddy, Olivia, and Jill began filling Doc in on the plans they'd made, but Val's mind kept wandering. She'd kept Pedro in the background of her thoughts until now, because the memory of how the burro had suffered made her so sad and angry. How she wished Doc would let them keep him! She knew it wasn't possible, but she wished it just the same. Teddy was right — Pedro was just the right size for him, and Erin, too. But first they'd have to tame him. Val didn't even want to think the word "break." That dreadful Mr. Wetzel had almost broken him, all right. But he hadn't broken Pedro's spirit.

It must have been awful for the little burro, Val thought, to be rounded up with lots of other wild burros and mustangs and taken from their home on the Western Plains. And then to be adopted by somebody like Wetzel, who had treated him so cruelly!

I bet I could tame him, Val thought. I'd be kind to him, and I'd never, ever beat him. Why, maybe I could teach him to let little children ride on his back, and we could take him to the Country Fair! And then maybe somebody nice would adopt him and give him a really good home. Val liked Wildlife Farm. It was clean and well-kept, and the animals there were happy and had plenty to eat. Gigi, the little monkey, and Leo the lion cub were fat and sassy, and all the visitors to Wildlife Farm loved them. There had been no other place to take them, once Doc had restored them to health after Mr. Zefferelli's Kosmic Karnival had abandoned them at Animal Inn. Nobody had been willing to adopt two such exotic animals, particularly not an animal like Leo, who was growing very fast into an honest-to-goodness lion.

But Wildlife Farm wasn't the right place for Pedro. Pedro needed lots of tender loving care, and someone who would treat him like a member of the family.

Like us, Val thought.

"Vallie, tell Dad about the pet show," Erin was saying. Val brought herself back to the present, and described her idea for Doc. He approved wholeheartedly, and Val drifted back into thoughts about Pedro.

She could just see him, his gray-brown coat all smooth and shining, his long, furry ears standing straight up instead of laid back in anger and fear, his neat little hooves trimmed and polished, not overgrown and cracked as they were now. She'd be leading him around on Miss Maggie's lawn, with a happy little child sitting on his back. Parents would pay at least a dollar to give their kids a donkey ride, Val was sure. Dozens of donkey rides — maybe hundreds! Hundreds of dollars to help build a new animal shelter for the Humane Society. . . .

"Vallie, are you still with us?"

Doc's voice cut into Val's thoughts.

"Oh, yes, Dad. I've just been thinking about Pedro," she said, carefully removing the striped kitten from her leg. It was rapidly making its way up her jeans, heading for her sweat shirt. It gave an indignant squeak when she picked it up and put it back on the floor with its brothers and sisters.

"Dad's going to ask Mrs. Racer if she'll bake some of her super cookies for the Fair," Teddy said. "And maybe her friends will, too. And you remember that quilt she told us about — the one she and the other Mennonite ladies have been working on? Well, maybe she'd let us auction it off. That oughta bring in a lot of bucks!"

Val nodded. "She probably will, Teddy. We'll ask her when she comes to work on Tuesday."

Doc sat down beside her and put an arm around her shoulders. "Vallie, I hope you're not making lots of plans about how we'll adopt Pedro, because it isn't going to happen. I'm as concerned about him as you are, but we can't keep him. You do know that, don't you?"

Val leaned her head against Doc's chest. "Yes, I know. Honest, I do. But while he's at Animal Inn, you wouldn't object if I tried to tame him, would you?"

"No, I wouldn't object to that. But try not to get too attached to him. Sooner or later, we'll have to find him a good home. And that home is not going to be ours."

"I know," Val repeated. "A good home — that's all I want for him."

A good home. But where, and with whom?

That was something she was going to have to figure out.

Chapter 6

The next day in the Hamilton Junior High cafeteria, Val and Jill were having lunch with their friends and talking about the Country Fair.

"We need all the help we can get," Val said. "And the first thing we have to do is spread the word about the Fair. It's going to be the first Saturday in June, at Miss Maggie Rafferty's place. That's only a few weeks away, so we'll need lots of posters all over town."

"I'll make some posters," said Alison Chase, and Jill quickly wrote her name down under "Publicity" in her notebook. Alison was a talented artist. She always won first prize in the annual Hamilton art show.

"I'll write an article for the *Sentinel*," Marty Greene said. She was a reporter for the school paper. "It's too late for this week's issue, but I'll put it on the front page next week."

Jill added her name to the list.

Val's friend Sarah Jones munched thoughtfully

on a corn chip. Sarah and Val played on the Hamilton girls' softball team, the Raiders.

"I can't draw, and I'm not much good at writing, either," she admitted. "But I'd like to help." Suddenly she brightened. "Hey, the one thing I *am* good at is sports. I bet people would pay to see a softball game — not just an ordinary game — but a special one."

Val frowned. "*How* special, Sarah? If we're going to charge admission, we'll have to give people their money's worth."

Sarah ate some more corn chips, thinking hard. Then, "I've got it!" she cried. "Girls against boys! The Raiders against the Buccaneers! A girls' team has never played a boys' team in the history of Hamilton Junior High. It'll be a sellout!"

"I love it!" Val said, and the other girls enthusiastically agreed. "But do you think Ms. Conklin and Mr. Weston will go for it? They're the coaches — it'll really be up to them."

"Sure they will," Sarah said. "You know how Ms. Conklin's always saying that the Raiders are a much stronger team than the Bucks. Well, this will be her chance to prove it. And if she challenges Mr. Weston, he won't dare back down." She grinned. "I bet we win, too! Ms. Conklin's probably in her office right now. I'll nab her before she goes to gym class."

Sarah grabbed her tray and hurried off, as Jill, after some hesitation as to how she should list Sarah, started a new column headed "Sports."

Marty was making notes, too. "This'll make great copy for my article," she said.

"Better wait until we find out if it's okay with the coaches," Val advised.

Marty looked up. "Naturally," she said. "The *Sentinel* never prints anything without the facts to back it up. In the meantime, I'm going to do a rough draft so when Sarah gives us the green light, I can go ahead."

"There's another very important thing you ought to put in that article, Marty," Val said. "And on your posters, too, Alison. It's the Humane Society's Adopt-A-Pet program. Until the Society finds another place to use as a shelter, there's nowhere in Essex to house homeless animals."

"Except Animal Inn," Jill put in.

"Whatever you do, *don't* mention Animal Inn in the article or on the posters!" Val said quickly. "We've got more animals than we can handle already. Other people have taken in a lot of the cats and dogs that lived at the shelter before the fire, but they can't keep them indefinitely. We have to make everyone aware of the problem, and ask them to adopt an animal if they possibly can. I'll get the phone number of the Humane Society office so you can list it for people to call."

"Val has three kittens that need homes," Jill added. "Yesterday there were four, but I took one home and my parents are going to let me keep her. What about you, Alison? Wouldn't you like an adorable, cuddly little kitten?"

"*I* would, but my brother's allergic to cats," Alison said. "He'd sneeze the house down if I brought one home."

Before Jill and Val could tackle Marty, she said, "Don't look at *me*! My cat just had kittens, and pretty soon we'll be putting them up for adoption. Hey, maybe I could bring them to the Country Fair. They'll be old enough to leave their mother by then."

"That's not a bad idea," said Val. "We could have a Kitty Corral — "

" — and a Puppy Pen," Jill said quickly. Her eyes lit up. "You know, maybe we could sell some of them! How about fifty cents for a kitten and seventy-five cents for a puppy?"

"Jill, we can't even *give* all these animals away," Val said patiently. "What makes you think people would actually *buy* them?"

Jill shrugged. "It was just a thought. And you know, Val, some people figure that unless they pay for something, it's not worth anything. But if they don't pay very much, they think they've got a real bargain. That's it!'' she cried. "We'll make signs — 'Cats and Kittens Five Dollars — Reduced to Fifty Cents for Quick Sale!' "

"Jill Dearborne, you're bananas," Marty said, standing up and picking up her tray. "Come on, Alison, we'll be late for class."

"Some people have no imagination," Jill sighed. "Guess we'd better be going, too."

The girls were on their way out of the cafeteria, when Val heard a familiar voice calling her name. . . . Familiar, but not welcome.

"Wait up, Val," Lila Bascombe called, hurrying toward Val and Jill.

Jill made a face. "What do you suppose Princess Lila wants?"

"Search me," Val said. "But you can bet she wants *something*. The only time Lila lowers herself to speak to us peasants is when she's after something."

"Whatever it is, let's say no!" Jill giggled, and Val grinned.

"I'm with you," she said.

Lila came up to them, accompanied as usual by her two closest friends, Kimberly and Courtney. They went everywhere together. Jill called them the Siamese Triplets. Lila was the leader of a crowd of girls who considered themselves very sophisticated, and they looked down on Val, Jill, and their friends. Lila was one of the very few people Val had ever met whom she didn't like and the feeling was mutual. Lila had never forgiven Val for getting her into trouble with her parents a while back — trouble that Lila richly deserved. But now here she was, smiling sweetly. Kimberly and Courtney were smiling, too. With an effort, Val smiled back.

"What's up, Lila?" she asked.

"I just wanted to tell you that I saw your picture in the *Gazette* yesterday morning. Too bad you didn't have time to fix your hair . . ." Lila paused, then finished, ". . . but come to think of it, that's the way it always looks, doesn't it?"

Val kept smiling. It wasn't easy. "I appreciate your concern for my appearance, Lila," she said, "but we're on our way to class, so if you have something else to say, make it snappy, okay?"

"Well, really!" Lila tossed her head. "You're awfully touchy today. It just so happens that I *do* have something else to say, something I think you'll want to hear."

"Spit it out, Lila," Jill snapped.

Lila pretended Jill hadn't spoken. "Kimberly, Courtney, and I are going to volunteer to help out with the Humane Society Country Fair," she said, and the other two girls nodded in unison. They seemed to be waiting for Val and Jill to react with astonishment and delight. They were disappointed.

"That's nice," Val said. "How come?"

Lila scowled. "What do you mean, 'how come?' It's a good cause, and we want to do our bit to help the poor homeless animals."

Val didn't believe a word of it. "Since when are you interested in animal welfare?" she asked. She remembered very well how Lila had tried to pass off Val's prize-winning essay in the Humane Society contest as her own, and Val knew that Lila didn't really care about anybody's welfare but Lila's.

"Honestly, Val, if this is the way you treat people who want to help, the Country Fair is going to be a disaster!" Lila said irritably.

Val had to admit she had a point. The important thing was the success of the Fair, not her personal feelings about Lila Bascombe.

"I'm sorry, Lila," she said. "I'm glad you and Courtney and Kimberly want to become involved. But how did you hear about it, anyway? We only decided to do it yesterday."

Lila sighed. "It's my great-aunt. She's very active in the Humane Society, and she called my parents last night to tell them she expected all of us to volunteer. She got Daddy to say he'd make a contribution, and Mother and my sister Lauren will help out on the day of the Fair. That left me, and Daddy absolutely insisted that I talk to you. He wants to stay on Great-aunt Maggie's good side. . . . After all, we're her only relatives, and she can't live forever. . . ."

"Wait a minute!" Val said. "Are you talking about Miss Maggie Rafferty?"

"Yes," Lila said, looking embarrassed and uncomfortable. "She's my father's aunt. Personally, I can't stand the old witch, but like I said, Daddy doesn't want her to cut him out of her will. She's filthy rich, even though she looks like something the cat dragged in."

It was very hard for Val to keep her temper. "Miss Maggie is a very wonderful person," she said. "So what if she's a little eccentric? You should be proud that she's your relative!"

"Oh, Val, you're such a bleeding heart!" Lila's smile was infuriatingly superior. "Just give me a straight answer. Can we help out with the Country Fair? Kimberly, Courtney, and I know exactly what we want to do."

"Yes, you can help," Val said from between clenched teeth. "What did you have in mind?"

"A fashion show," Lila said promptly.

"A *fashion show*?" Jill echoed. "At a Country Fair?"

"Why not? It'll attract a higher class of people. People with more money," Lila told her coolly. "My mother is a very good customer at all the best clothing stores in town, and she's sure they'll donate some outfits to be sold for the benefit of the Humane Society. Of course, Courtney, Kimberly, and I will be the models."

"Of course," Val said weakly. She caught Jill's eye. Jill raised her eyebrows, but didn't say a word.

"Then it's settled. I'll tell my mother to talk to Brenda of Brenda's Boutique, and she'll contact The Style Shoppe and Fashion Unlimited, too. Don't worry, Val." Lila patted Val's arm. "We'll take care of everything. The fashion show will be the hit of the Fair, just you wait and see."

She and her friends moved off down the hall, leaving Val and Jill staring after them.

"A fashion show?" Jill repeated, shaking her head. "Are you out of your mind, Val? We need a fashion show like we need a hole in the head — *both* our heads!"

"It's not the worst idea in the world," Val said. "Lila may be right — it may attract people who wouldn't otherwise come to the Fair. And at least it will get Lila's crowd involved. Who knows? It might even make some money." As they headed for their first afternoon class, she added, "What really blows my mind is that Miss Maggie is Lila's great-aunt! I never met two people who were as different as Lila and Miss Maggie. I could have *killed* Lila for talking that way about her! The Bascombes are just sitting around, waiting for Miss Maggie to die so they can inherit her money. I hope Miss Maggie lives forever!"

"From what I've seen of Miss Maggie, she probably will," Jill said. "Or maybe she'll leave all her money to the Humane Society. Now *that* would knock their socks off!"

"Lauren's different, though," Val mused. Lauren was Lila's college-aged sister. "She's not like Lila at all. If Miss Maggie leaves her money to anybody in that family, she ought to leave it to Lauren — only I hope it's not going to happen for a long, long time."

"Is Miss Maggie really all that rich?" Jill asked.

"I guess she must be. She has that big house and all those grounds. But she doesn't spend much of anything on herself. She makes lots of donations to charities, not just to the Humane Society. Miss Maggie really cares about the underdog."

"And the under*cat*, too," Jill said with a giggle. "I wonder if Miss Maggie knows what kind of a person her great-niece really is?"

"I'll bet she does," Val said. "And I bet that's why she insisted that Lila help out with the fund-raiser. Maybe she thinks that doing something for somebody else will make Lila less self-centered."

"Ha! If that's what she thinks, Miss Maggie really *does* have a couple of screws loose!" Jill caught the scowl Val aimed at her, and added quickly, "Just kidding, Val, just kidding!"

* * *

As soon as classes were over for the day, Val hopped on her bike and pedaled off for Animal Inn. Doc didn't have office hours on Mondays, so she didn't have to work, but she was eager to ride The Ghost, and to see how Pedro was getting along.

The Ghost was as happy as she was to be trotting along the deserted country roads beneath tall trees that were budding with tiny, tender green leaves. Farmers were plowing their fields, and in the pastures, leggy, awkward colts were frisking by contented mares. Val saw lambs and calves playing in fields that were covered with sweet grass. The air was soft and pure. Early wildflowers sprinkled the banks between which Val and The Ghost passed.

Val thought of Pedro, and her heart ached for the little burro. He ought to be enjoying the beauty of spring, but instead he stood in the stall next to The Ghost, mad at the world.

Val had stopped by to say hello to Pedro and to offer him an apple, one of two she'd brought from home. But Pedro had paid no attention to her, and when she'd tried to pat him, he'd laid back his ears and kicked.

"It's gonna take a while for that donkey to understand that nobody wants to hurt him," Mike had told her sadly. "I talked to him a lot last night — tried to explain that he's safe now, that he ain't gonna be beaten no more. But he can't believe it, Vallie.

I'd like to get my hands on John Wetzel! I knowed him when he was a kid, and he was a bad kid way back then — the kinda boy who'd rip the wings off flies and laugh to see them stagger around till they died. Didn't like him then and don't like him now."

"Do you think he'll ever trust us, Mike?" Val asked. "If we can tame him, I know we can find him a home. But if he keeps biting and kicking, nobody will ever take him, not even Wildlife Farm."

"Give him time, Vallie," Mike said. "That's all he needs — time. He's young and he's strong. If he wasn't strong, he'd've died long ago. Just be patient."

But it was very hard to be patient, especially on a beautiful day like this.

Val reached down and patted The Ghost's neck. Sunshine and fresh air and sweet green grass — Pedro deserved all of these. And when the time was right, he'd be able to enjoy them. But right now, that time seemed very far away.

Chapter
7

"My lands! What have we got here?" said Mrs. Racer as she came through the door on Tuesday morning. The three kittens were perched on various pieces of furniture — the striped one on the back of the big wing chair by the fireplace, the black-and-white one on the desk, and the gray one on an arm of the sofa. Jocko and Sunshine had come to greet her, then raced off to bark at first one kitten, then another.

"Somebody dumped them at Animal Inn," Val said. "Jocko, stop that! I can't hear myself think. Sunshine, leave Two alone!"

"There used to be four, but Jill took one," Teddy said, running over to give Mrs. Racer a hug. "Wouldn't you like a kitten, Mrs. Racer? I'm taking Two to school today for show-and-tell, and I bet somebody will adopt him. You could have One or Three."

Mrs. Racer looked puzzled. "I couldn't take three if you're taking two to school, Teddy. That leaves one."

"One *and* Three," Teddy corrected. "I'm taking Two, so One and Three are left."

"I think you ought to take only one, Teddy," said Mrs. Racer. "And if you take one, that leaves two, not one and three. One and three are four."

"I don't want to take One — he's crazy. Dad said I could take Two. Three's all right, but Erin thinks maybe Olivia will take her, unless you want Three."

By now Mrs. Racer was totally confused. "Teddy, I never said I'd take any of them. I surely won't be able to take *three*."

"You don't understand, Mrs. Racer," Erin giggled. "We couldn't think of names for the kittens right away, so we gave them numbers. The stripey one is Two, the gray one is One, and the black-and-white one is Three."

"So wouldn't you like to take Three home with you?" Teddy asked hopefully.

Mrs. Racer shook her head in amazement. "Well, I never! My goodness, this family gets stranger and stranger. Numbered cats!"

Val picked up Three and handed her to Mrs. Racer. "Why don't you two get acquainted?" she suggested. "I know you'll like her, and you told me when Mose died last summer you were thinking of getting a kitten." Mose was Mrs. Racer's orange cat, and he was Cleveland's father.

As Mrs. Racer held and stroked the kitten, Erin

suddenly cried, "Oh, rats! The button just popped off my skirt. Mrs. Racer, could you sew it on for me?"

"Mrs. Racer, do you remember where I put my spiral notebook?" Teddy asked, dropping to his hands and knees and peering under the sofa. "Oh, hi, Cleveland. Vallie, Cleveland's hiding under the sofa."

"Well, drag him out," Val sighed. "Maybe if I put him in the pantry I can get him to eat something."

"Erin, bring me the sewing basket so I can fix your skirt. Teddy, last time I saw that notebook it was on top of the television set. Vallie, what's the matter with Cleveland? Is he sick?"

Mrs. Racer sat in the rocker and began threading a needle. Three settled down comfortably in her lap.

"Not sick, just jealous," Val said, taking the cat from Teddy. "You know how he gets whenever we bring a new animal into the house. All he does is sulk, and he's been on a hunger strike since Sunday when we brought the kittens home."

"You just leave Cleveland to me," said Mrs. Racer. "I'll give him some nice leftover chicken. That'll perk him up."

Val carried Cleveland into the kitchen and dumped him in the pantry next to his bowl of cat food. She ignored the dirty look he gave her as she closed the door.

"Mrs. Racer, can you hurry, please?" Erin begged. "I don't want to be late for school."

"Dad's driving us, so we have time," Teddy said. "That's because I can't take Two on the school bus. Vallie, where's the cat carrier?"

"In the basement. Did you find your notebook?"

"Yep. Got it!" Teddy dashed off to get the cat carrier.

As Val put her books into her knapsack, she said, "Mrs. Racer, did you hear about the fire at the animal shelter?"

"Indeed I did," Mrs. Racer said. "M'son Henry showed me the picture on the front page of the *Gazette*. The article said that you and Doc saved a lot of animals' lives. I was so proud, I thought I'd bust!"

Val beamed. "It was mostly Dad, but I helped a little. The problem is, all those animals are at Animal Inn now, and it's so crowded that we don't have room for any more patients. The Humane Society's sponsoring a Country Fair to help raise money for a new shelter, and we thought maybe you'd bake some of your super cookies to sell."

"Of course I will!" Mrs. Racer finished sewing on the button and gave Erin back her skirt. "I'll get some of my friends to help me."

"That's great!" Val said. "Thanks so much." She

gave Mrs. Racer a quick kiss, then glanced at her watch. "Gee, I have to run." She slung her backpack over her shoulder and grabbed her jacket. "See you tonight, Mrs. Racer." She went to the foot of the stairs in the hall and called, " 'Bye, Dad. See you later."

" 'Bye, Vallie. Have a good day," Doc called back.

As Val went out the door, she heard Teddy yelling from the basement, "Mrs. Racer! I can't find the cat carrier. Can you help me look?"

"Coming, Teddy." Mrs. Racer stood up, holding Three in one hand. "How you all manage when I'm not here, I'll never know," she said happily.

"Vallie! Look out for One!" Erin cried. Val quickly leaned down and picked up the little gray kitten as it dashed between her feet. She handed it to Erin.

"Try to persuade Olivia to take One," Val said. "I think Mrs. Racer's probably going to adopt Three."

"I'll see what I can do, but she really likes Three better," said Erin.

"*Try*," Val called as she mounted her bike.

When Val arrived at Animal Inn after school, she saw a beat-up bicycle leaning against a tree by the parking lot. She recognized it right away. It belonged to Miss Maggie Rafferty. Miss Maggie was the only person in Essex who rode a twenty-five-year-old Schwinn with balloon tires. She could have afforded a Rolls Royce, but Miss Maggie hated cars and had never learned to drive. She went everywhere on her old Schwinn.

Val hoped Miss Maggie hadn't come to report another case of animal abuse — one bruised and battered burro was all Val could handle.

"What's Miss Maggie doing here?" Val asked Pat Dempwolf, Doc's receptionist, as she stowed her backpack and jacket behind the desk in the waiting room.

"She came to check on the animals that were injured in the fire," Pat told her. "What a terrible thing that was! It's a miracle none of the animals died."

"It sure was," Val agreed. "If it wasn't for Dad, Miss Maggie, and George Frick, we would have lost some for sure."

"And you, too, Vallie. Look on the bulletin board," Pat said, smiling.

Val looked at the bulletin board behind the desk, and there was the picture from Sunday's paper, pinned up with four bright red thumbtacks. She couldn't help blushing, particularly when she read the hand-lettered sign Pat had posted above the picture. It said: OUR HEROES.

"Oh, dear," she said faintly.

"Well, you *are*," Pat announced, and several pet owners in the waiting room enthusiastically agreed.

"Uh, guess I'd better get to work," Val mumbled. She took a fresh white lab coat from the closet behind Pat and went into the treatment room. Toby was holding down a cocker spaniel while Doc prepared to give the dog its five-in-one-shot.

"Hi, hero," Toby said, grinning.

"Cut it out, Toby!" Val's cheeks were still pink. "What can I do to help, Dad?"

"It's time for afternoon medications, Vallie," Doc said. "Check the charts and give the animals their medicine. You might say hello to Miss Maggie, too. I left her in the infirmary. She stopped by to pay a call on the fire victims."

Val studied the charts on the clipboard hanging on the wall by the door, gathered up the proper medications, and went into the infirmary. The first thing she saw was Miss Maggie, bending over so that she was eye-to-eye with the bald cat. As usual, Miss Maggie was wearing an oversized shirt, baggy fatigue pants — secured with bicycle clips, and desert boots. Her wild salt-and-pepper hair was twisted into an untidy knot that looked as if it might come down any minute.

As Val entered, Miss Maggie straightened up.

"Thomas appears to be doing nicely," she said. "Too bad about his fur and whiskers. He was a handsome cat — will be again — once everything grows back. Need a hand?"

"Hello, Miss Maggie. You don't have to help me — I'm just giving everybody their medicine and ointment and stuff," Val said.

"I know I don't *have* to," Miss Maggie snapped. "Do you want a hand? Yes or no?"

"Uh, yes, sure." Val checked her chart. "Thomas gets an antibiotic tablet and some ointment on his burns."

"Fine. I'll hold him while you give him his pill. Then I'll put the ointment on while you take care of the next patient."

Miss Maggie opened Thomas's cage and lifted the cat out briskly but gently. She pinched Thomas's jaws to make him open his mouth, and when Val popped the pill down his throat, Miss Maggie rubbed his throat to help him swallow. It was obvious she knew what she was doing.

"How are Calico and her kittens?" Val asked, handing Miss Maggie the ointment and going on to the next cage.

"Whole family's doing well. Speaking of family, did my bubble-headed great-niece speak to you yet?" Miss Maggie asked.

It took Val a moment to realize who she was talking about. "You mean Lila? Yes, she did. She and her friends volunteered to help with the Country Fair."

"Glad to hear it. Do the girl good to think about something besides herself for a change," Miss Maggie said. "Here, let me hold Brownie. He's blind in one eye, and if you approach him from the left and he doesn't see you, he might snap."

Miss Maggie put Thomas back into his cage and got a firm grip on the big mongrel with the broken leg.

"What's Lila going to do for the Fair?" she asked.

"Well, she wants to model fancy clothes in a fashion show," Val said, smoothing ointment on Brownie's ear.

Miss Maggie snorted. Val thought she sounded just like The Ghost. "That's Lila, all right! Always wants to be the center of attention. Don't know what I've done to deserve such unsatisfactory relatives. Greedy, too. They're just sitting around, waiting for me to cork off so they can spend my money. But I'll tell you this, they're going to have a mighty long wait!"

"I hope so," Val said. She gave Brownie a pat and closed the door of his cage, then moved on to the next.

"Only good apple in the barrel is Lauren," Miss Maggie went on. "Maybe I'll leave everything to her. That'd make them sit up and take notice!" She glanced at Val out of eyes that were a startling, sparkling blue. "Guess you think I'm morbid, talking this way. Well, I'm not. Just planning ahead, you might say." Suddenly she grinned. "You think I'm a crazy old woman, don't you?'' Before Val could speak, she went on, ''I probably am, but that's my business.'' She held another cat while Val gave it a pill. ''Remember I told you your father looks like an Airedale I had once?''

Val nodded, smiling.

''People always remind me of animals. Take you, for instance. You remind me of a sturdy brown pony. Are you insulted?''

Val laughed. ''Oh, no! I love horses and ponies. If I could be any animal in the world, I'd like to be a horse. What kind of animal do you think Toby looks like?''

''Who's Toby?'' Miss Maggie asked, returning the cat to its cage.

''The boy who works here with me.'' Val went on to the next cage.

''Oh, yes. The one with the curly hair and big ears. Let's see . . . a springer spaniel, I think. Yes, that's it.''

Val couldn't resist asking, ''What about Lila?''

Miss Maggie snorted again. ''That's easy. A yappy little French poodle, the kind with bows on its ears and pink polish on its toenails.''

Val was laughing so hard she could barely manage to give the little schnauzer its medicine. ''Miss Maggie, you're terrible!'' she cried.

''Yes, I am,'' Miss Maggie agreed cheerfully. ''When you're as old as I am, you can be terrible if you like. It's one of the advantages of age. I say what I think, and I don't care about anybody's opinion. It helps to be rich, too," she added. "Rich people can do pretty much as they like, no matter how old they are."

"If you're so rich, Miss Maggie, how come you don't spend any money on yourself?" Val asked. The minute the words were out of her mouth, Val wished she hadn't said them. But somehow, talking to Miss Maggie made her speak her mind without thinking.

"Good question." Miss Maggie nodded approvingly. "You mean why don't I dress like a proper old lady and ride in a chauffeured limousine, and have servants to wait on me so I don't have to lift a finger? Because it's boring, that's why. I told you, rich people can do what they like, and I like to wear men's trousers, cook my own meals, and ride my bicycle. And I like to take care of animals and give money to worthwhile charities, like the Humane Society. I could have spent five thousand dollars on a coat made from the skins of helpless little minks, but instead I wrote a check to the Society to help finance a new shelter. I don't need a mink coat. Nobody *needs* a mink coat. But these animals need somewhere to live. By the way, Valentine, I've cleared out the old stable behind my house — spent the past two days doing it. When the animals you're caring for are ready to leave, you tell young Theodore to bring them over to me. They can stay in the stable until there's somewhere else to put them."

"Oh, Miss Maggie, that's wonderful!" Val cried. She couldn't quite get used to hearing her father referred to as "young Theodore," but she realized that to someone as old as Miss Maggie, Doc must seem very young indeed.

"It's not wonderful. It's what I want to do, and I always do what I want. Now let's take a look at that burro, if we're finished here."

Val checked her charts. All the animals in the infirmary had been accounted for. "Pedro's in the Large Animal Clinic," she said, leading the way.

They found Pedro standing in a corner of his stall. When they leaned over the door, he switched his tail and flattened his long, furry ears.

"He doesn't like people much," Val told Miss Maggie.

"Don't blame him. Neither do I."

Miss Maggie gazed at the burro for a long time. "John Wetzel ought to be shot," she said at last. "I'd shoot him myself if it wasn't against the law."

"Me, too," Val said.

"John Wetzel was a nasty little boy when he was one of my pupils fifty years ago," Miss Maggie said. "He's grown up to be a nasty man. Do what you can for Pedro, Valentine. He needs all the help he can get."

"I will," Val promised.

Miss Maggie turned her bright blue gaze on Val. "I always liked sturdy little ponies," she said, smiling. The smile widened. "What kind of an animal do I remind you of?"

Val thought about it for a moment. The image that came into her head was sharp and clear.

"A horse. A thoroughbred jumper, like The Gray Ghost."

Miss Maggie laughed. Her laugh was like a whinny.

"Very good, Valentine! Very good indeed!"

Chapter
8

It seemed to Val that the next two weeks galloped by so fast that she could hardly believe it. Plans for the Country Fair were in full swing. The telephone never stopped ringing both at Animal Inn and at the Taylors' home, as members of Doc's committee checked in with progress reports. Val and Toby met with their junior committee once a week at Val's house, usually on a Sunday afternoon, fueled by dozens of Mrs. Racer's cookies and pitchers of ice-cold milk. Much to Val's surprise, Lila even attended a few of the meetings and gave detailed reports on each and every outfit that had been donated for the fashion show.

Toby was putting up posters and flyers all over his school, and announced that Mr. Curran planned to set up a tent on Miss Maggie's property where Curran's ice cream would be sold. All proceeds would be donated to the Humane Society's building fund. Marty's front page article in the Hamilton *Sentinel* was followed by updates every week, and the softball game between the Raiders and the Buccaneers was the talk of the school. Teddy, Erin, and their friends at Jackson spread the word from kindergarten through the sixth grade. Their teachers even held a contest for the best Country Fair poster. Jill's list of volunteers and projects took up several pages in her notebook.

At Animal Inn, the space problem was easing up a little, since Miss Maggie, true to her word, took each fire victim as soon as it was better and gave it a temporary home in her stable. And at the Taylors' house, Cleveland was a slightly happier cat since only one kitten was left. Olivia had been persuaded to adopt little gray One, and one of Teddy's classmates had talked his parents into letting him have Two. Though Mrs. Racer was very fond of Three, she still hadn't agreed to take her home, but Val was sure it was only a matter of time before she weakened.

The big problem that remained was Pedro. No matter how hard she tried, Val couldn't seem to get through to him. His health had improved, his wounds were healed, but his disposition hadn't gotten any sweeter with the passage of time. When Val offered him an apple or a carrot, he either ignored her or tried to nip her fingers. If she tried to pet him, he jerked away as though she had a whip in her hand.

"Maybe he just doesn't like *me*," she said sadly to Toby late one afternoon. The burro stood as far away from Val as he could get, pretending she wasn't there.

"It's not you, Val," Toby told her. "He doesn't like anybody. He doesn't even like The Ghost, and you'd think they'd be pals since they've been next door neighbors for weeks now."

Val sighed. "I know. And it hurts The Ghost's feelings just exactly the way it does mine, I can tell. I just hope that awful Wetzel hasn't ruined Pedro for life. I'm sure Pedro wasn't a bad animal when Wetzel got him, but maybe Wetzel turned him into one. . . ." Then she shook her head. "No! I can't believe that. I don't believe there is such a thing as a bad animal. There must be a way to show Pedro we don't mean him any harm."

"That's exactly what I been tellin' him." Mike came up beside Val and Toby, Ludwig trotting at his heels. Val was surprised to see the German shepherd. In spite of his protests, Mike had taken Ludwig home with him, and Val hadn't seen him for weeks. "I talk to Pedro a lot at night, after you all go home," Mike went on, "but he don't have much to say for himself. I tell him nobody's ever gonna hurt him again, but I guess he don't believe me." Mike looked sad. He was very proud of his ability to communicate with animals, and this was the first time he'd failed.

Val bent down to pat Ludwig. The dog looked sad, too, she thought.

"What's Ludwig doing here?" she asked Mike. "He's not sick, is he? He looks kind of droopy."

"Dunno what's wrong with him," Mike said. "I been kinda worried about him lately, to tell you the truth. Thought maybe Doc oughta check him out, but your dad says there's nothing wrong with him, 'cept maybe old age. But he ain't even that old — no more'n seven or eight, Doc thinks."

Ludwig lay down at Mike's feet, gave a sigh, and rested his gray muzzle between his paws.

"Cheer up, Ludwig. What've you got to look so sorrowful about?" Toby asked.

Ludwig wagged his tail once and closed his eyes.

"Maybe he needs a shrink," Toby suggested.

"Oh, Toby, be serious!" cried Val.

"No, really. I was reading somewhere that there are psychiatrists for animals just like there are for people. Maybe Pedro needs one, too."

"That donkey don't need no head doctor," Mike said. "What he needs is a friend."

"But Pedro has friends, lots of friends," Val said. "He has us, and The Ghost would be his friend if he'd let him."

"Well," said Mike, "guess I better get on with my work. Gotta clean out Pedro's stall, if he don't kick me into the middle of next week."

"Be careful, Mike," Val warned as Mike picked up a pitchfork and opened the gate. Before he could step inside, Ludwig ambled past him.

"Uh-oh," Toby said. "Better get Ludwig out of there!"

Trying to stay away from the burro's hindquarters, Mike reached for Ludwig's collar. But the big dog just walked straight up to Pedro and whined softly.

"Ludwig!" Mike called. "Come here! That donkey's gonna send you flying!"

Pedro looked over his shoulder, and one long, furry ear slowly came forward. Ludwig whined again, and Pedro's other ear joined the first.

"What's he saying, Mike?" Val asked.

"Beats me," Mike said. "But seems like Pedro's listening."

Ludwig's tail was wagging gently. Pedro turned around and stretched out his neck until his nose was almost touching Ludwig's. The German shepherd's long pink tongue licked Pedro's nose. The burro didn't back away.

"Will you look at that now," Mike said wonderingly. "Don't that beat all!"

"It looks like Pedro's found a friend at last," Val said.

"Ludwig looks a lot happier, too," Toby added. "Maybe he thinks Pedro's a big, overgrown dog."

"And maybe Pedro thinks Ludwig's a small burro," Val giggled.

Leaning on the handle of his pitchfork, Mike

mused, "You know, could be the trouble with Ludwig's been that he's lonely for other animals. Come to think of it, he was real happy baby-sitting for them pups of yours, Toby."

Val reached into her hip pocket and took out a carrot. Very slowly, so as not to alarm Pedro, she came into the stall and moved to within about a foot of him. She stroked Ludwig's head with one hand and stretched out the other with the carrot on her open palm. Pedro raised his head, looking at Val with his big brown eyes. His ears flicked once or twice, but he didn't flatten them in anger and fear. Tentatively he snuffled at the carrot. Val held her breath. Then he daintily lifted it from her palm with velvety lips and began munching. As he chewed, Val lightly touched his fuzzy neck. Pedro's hide quivered as though she were an annoying fly, but he didn't jerk away or try to nip her.

She looked over at Mike. "Do you think Ludwig could sleep over tonight?" she asked, smiling.

Mike grinned. "Don't see why not." He followed Val out of the stall and fastened the gate behind him. "I'll clean in here later on. Might as well let those two keep on getting acquainted." He gave Val a mock scowl. "But don't you try and talk me into takin' 'em *both* home with me tomorrow morning! Ain't got room in my place for a dog *and* a donkey!"

* * *

From that moment on, Pedro was a very different burro, and Ludwig was a much happier dog. The two were inseparable. Ludwig slept in Pedro's stall and trotted at his side like a proud parent when the burro was let out to join The Ghost in the pasture. Pedro no longer ignored or nipped at The Ghost when the big dapple gray horse tried to make friends, and Val often glanced out the window of Animal Inn to see Pedro, The Ghost, and Ludwig frolicking in the lush green grass.

At last, Val was able to put into operation her plan to train the little burro so that he could be ridden. Whenever she had some spare time, she petted him, gave him treats, and led him around the pasture by his halter. She had no saddle or bridle small enough to fit Pedro, so she and Toby fashioned a makeshift saddle from a folded blanket, which they secured around the burro's middle with a wide leather strap Toby had found. They tied a piece of lightweight rope from one side of his halter to the other to serve as reins.

Now all they needed was a rider. Val knew Teddy was dying to be first to ride Pedro, but she wasn't sure how the burro would react the first time someone sat on his back.

"How about using a dummy?" Toby suggested.

"You want to volunteer?" Val teased.

97

"Very funny. I mean some kind of weight, so he'll get used to the idea," Toby said. "How about one of those big sacks of pet food? They weigh fifty pounds, about as much as a little kid."

"That's not a bad idea. Come on, let's get one!" said Val.

Together, they loaded a sack of dog chow into Mike's wheelbarrow and Toby wheeled it out to the pasture. Then, while Val held onto Pedro, Toby hefted the sack onto Pedro's back. He danced around a little and snorted, but Val calmed him with soothing words and the offer of a big, fat carrot, and soon she was leading him around the pasture with no problem at all. The Ghost ambled along beside them, looking interested, and Ludwig trailed along behind.

As they passed Toby sitting on the fence, he called, "Hey, Val, look at Ludwig!"

She glanced over her shoulder to see the big German shepherd pausing every few steps to eat something on the ground.

"The bag sprung a leak!" Toby told her, laughing. "Looks like old Ludwig's getting the best of this deal!"

It was two weeks before the date of the Fair. Val and Toby decided that Pedro was ready to trade the feed sack for a real live rider. On a sunny late May afternoon, Teddy and his friends Eric, Billy, and Sparky, as well as Erin, Olivia, and Doc gathered by the pasture fence.

"Me first! Me first!" Teddy cried, jumping up and down. "And then Billy, and then Eric. . . ."

"And then me!" Sparky shouted, her freckled face alight with excitement. "I've never ridden a donkey before. I can have a ride, can't I, Vallie?"

"Sure you can, Sparky," Val said. It was hard to believe that this was the same tough little kid who'd blackened Teddy's eye a little more than a month ago, and who had been so terrified of The Ghost that it had taken all Val's powers of persuasion to make her ride him.

"I think you'd better let me hold onto you, Teddy," Doc said. "Pedro may have gotten used to having a feed sack on his back, but a bouncy little boy is something else."

"Oh, Dad, come on!" Teddy groaned. "What do you think I am, some dumb little kid or something?"

"Teddy, I know you're a rootin-tootin' cowboy who can break any bronco on the range," Doc said, "but this isn't the range, and Pedro isn't a bronco. He's just a little burro who's never been ridden before, and it's entirely possible he might not like the idea. If you don't want me to hold you, Sparky can have the first ride."

"You can hold me on, Doc," Sparky said, running over to him. "I'm not a scaredy-cat anymore, but I'd like you to hang onto me just in case."

"Hold it, Sparky!" Teddy shoved her out of the way. "Vallie said I could have the first ride, and I'm gonna do it, no matter what." He looked up at his father. "Okay, Dad. Give me a boost."

Doc lifted him onto Pedro's back. The burro quivered a little and danced around, but Val whispered into one long ear, and he calmed down. She began leading him across the pasture, with Doc holding Teddy firmly in place. As usual, Ludwig trotted beside them, wagging his tail.

By the time they returned to the waiting group, Doc had let go of Teddy.

"See? I told you I could do it!" Teddy cried, sliding off. "Nothing to it. Your turn, Billy."

When everyone had had a ride, Val turned to Doc, beaming with pride. "I told you we'd tamed him, Dad. Now will you let us sell donkey rides at the Country Fair?"

"So that's why you've been working so hard with Pedro," Doc said with a smile. "I don't see why not. He seems to be a reformed character. But shouldn't you share the credit for taming him, Vallie?"

"I said 'we,' " Val told him. "It wasn't just me. Toby helped, too."

"I know that," Doc said. "But what about your other helper, the four-legged one?"

"Oh, you mean Ludwig." Val patted the German shepherd's head. "You're right, Dad. We couldn't have done it without Ludwig. He's Pedro's very best friend."

"I like Ludwig," Sparky said, crouching down next to the dog and putting one sturdy arm around his neck. "I wish I could adopt him, but my mom says one cat is all she can handle, and Charlie doesn't like dogs much."

"Ludwig doesn't need to be adopted," Val said. "He belongs to Mike."

But she had a sudden chilling thought. If somebody decided to give Pedro a home, that would mean he'd be separated from Ludwig. He'd be unhappy without his friend, Val knew, and Ludwig would be unhappy without Pedro. It would be so nice if Doc would allow her to keep Pedro at Animal Inn, but that wasn't possible. He'd already spoken to the people at Wildlife Farm, and they were willing to take the burro, provided he was gentle enough for children to ride him. He was gentle enough, all right, but would he continue to be so without Ludwig?

Chapter
9

The night before the Country Fair, Val kept her fingers crossed tight (and her toes, too), hoping that the day would be fair and bright. The weather reports had all predicted sunshine and record temperatures in the high eighties, but Val knew that the forecasters sometimes made mistakes. If it rained, the Fair would be held the following Saturday. But it wouldn't be the same. People would forget or would have made other plans.

When she opened her eyes that morning, she was dazzled by the sunshine pouring through her window. There wasn't a cloud in the blue sky.

Val leaped out of bed, waking up Cleveland, too. The big orange cat stretched, yawned, and curled back into a furry ball.

"Come on, Cleveland," Val urged, poking him in the tummy. "I'm thinking of entering you in the Fattest Cat contest. How about a nice, big breakfast?"

"Vallie, you up?"

Erin poked her head around Val's door. "I just

took my shower. The bathroom's free. Better grab it before Daddy and Teddy do."

Val dashed for the bathroom. She had to shower, dress, and bike out to Animal Inn to get The Ghost ready for the parade. It was to form on Market Street, right in front of the court house, at nine o'clock, and it was already a quarter after seven.

Ten minutes later, Val was back in her bedroom, blow-drying her hair. She'd laid out the clothes she would wear the night before: jodhpurs, boots, a tattersall shirt, and the brown velvet hard hat she'd bought months ago. That was the kind of hat you wore when you rode a champion jumper like The Ghost, even if he couldn't jump anymore.

Val was nervous. There was no reason for her to be, but she was. Jill had coordinated all the activities of the junior committee, and everyone, even Lila, was well prepared. She was sure that the grown-ups were completely ready. The Humane Society float would be a big success, she knew. All the members of the fund-raising committee would be there, dressed in animal costumes. Mrs. Racer had been sewing away like mad on Doc's dog costume, and she and her friends had been baking hundreds of cookies.

"Vallie?"

Val heard the knock on the door and her father's voice.

"C'mon in," she called.

Doc entered. The moment she saw him, Val burst into laughter. He was wearing the dog suit, holding the headpiece in one hand.

"Not one word!" Doc said. "I know I look ridiculous. Wait till you see the head. Any self-respecting dog would laugh itself sick at the sight of me. But you're my daughter. Try to restrain yourself."

Doc put on the headpiece and Val laughed even harder. It was the ears that finished her off. They were so long and floppy!

"You're the biggest beagle I ever saw!" she gasped when she could speak. "Wait till Miss Maggie sees you. She won't think you look like an Airdale anymore."

"I am only doing this for the benefit of the Humane Society," Doc said with great dignity. "I may never live it down. We may have to move to another state."

He fumbled inside the dog suit and came up with a battered notebook. Flipping through the pages, he said, "According to my notes, we're in good shape. Everything okay on your end, Vallie?"

"Seems to be," Val said. "Teddy's cub scout leader is picking him up at eight-thirty, Erin and Olivia are riding their bikes in the parade, and I'm on my way out to saddle up The Ghost. Toby will meet me there — he's going to be riding Pedro. The rest of my committee will be at Miss Maggie's, setting up."

"All but one," Doc said.

"Really? Who?"

"Lila Bascombe. According to Miss Maggie, when Lila heard the Society was going to have a float, she begged and pleaded to be allowed to ride on it. Naturally, we couldn't refuse." Val could tell that Doc was trying very hard not to smile. He looked just the way Teddy did when he was up to mischief. "I get the impression that Lila pictures herself in frills and ruffles, tossing roses to the crowd, like a high school homecoming queen."

Val's eyes widened with devilish delight. "Didn't anybody tell her that everyone on the float has to wear an animal costume?" she asked.

"You know, come to think of it, I don't believe anybody did," said Doc. "I think she was told that the Society would provide her with something to wear. But fortunately, that's not my department. I take absolutely no responsibility for Lila, Lila's costume, or Lila's state of mind."

"Oh, boy!" Val cried happily. "This parade is going to be even more fun than I thought!"

Teddy dashed into the room, wearing pajama bottoms, his cub scout shirt, and his beloved Phillies baseball cap.

"Vallie, have you seen my — " he began. Then

he saw Doc, and collapsed on Val's bed, laughing so hard he couldn't stand up.

"I fail to see what's so amusing, young man," Doc said, pretending to glare at him. "Show a little respect for your elders and betters!"

When he finally sobered up enough to speak, Teddy said, "Gee, Dad, can I enter you in the pet contest? You'd win Biggest Dog, that's for sure!"

"How about Most Unusual Pet?" Val giggled.

Erin poked her head in the door. "I think Daddy looks cute," she said, grinning.

"I'm glad that *somebody* in this family has good taste," said Doc. He tucked his notebook back inside the dog suit. "Well, I'm off. I'll see all of you at the Square around a quarter to nine."

"Dad, are you going to drive?" Val asked.

"Well, I'm certainly not going to walk through town dressed like this," Doc said. "I'd probably be hauled into the pound — I don't have a dog license."

"Then you'd better take off your ears," Val suggested. "If other motorists see a dog driving a car, they might run right off the road!"

"Good idea, Vallie," Doc said. He took off the headpiece and stuffed it into one sleeve. "Don't know how dogs manage without pockets," he grumbled.

"Daddy, aren't you going to have any breakfast?" Erin asked.

"Don't have time. I'll pick up a bone on the way out."

Doc left, and the back view of him set Val, Teddy, and Erin off again.

"The ears are wonderful, but the tail's even better!" Val cried.

By the time Val and Toby reached the town square of Essex, they had collected quite a following of kids on bikes and on foot, and even some people in cars. Val sat tall and proud in the saddle, knowing that The Ghost looked every inch the champion he was. She'd curried and brushed him until his coat gleamed like satin. Toby had groomed Pedro within an inch of his life, too, but Toby was suffering agonies of embarrassment. Val had never seen his ears so red. He hadn't wanted to ride Pedro because his long legs hung down on either side of the burro until his feet almost touched the ground.

"I look ridiculous," he'd muttered as they prepared to leave Animal Inn. "Besides, I'm too heavy for him."

"No, you're not," Val had replied cheerfully. "Burros can carry close to three hundred pounds, and you don't weigh nearly that much. As for looking ridiculous, wait till you see Dad!"

"What do you mean?" Toby asked, but Val

wouldn't tell him. All she'd say was, "Have you ever seen a six-foot-tall beagle?"

"Very funny!"

But Toby had been a good sport, in spite of the comments that were shouted at him as he rode along.

"Hey, kid, why don't you let that donkey ride *you*?"

"He's not really riding at all — he's walking!"

"Hey, kid, why don't you pick on somebody your own size?"

The minute they reached the square, Toby got off and began attaching the signs he'd made on either side of Pedro's blanket-saddle: GIVE THIS BURRO A HOME, the signs said. He kept his head lowered, hoping that the kids in his school band, who were marching in the parade, wouldn't recognize him.

The town square was filled with the participants in the parade and onlookers eager for it to start. Val thought she'd never seen such chaos, or heard such noise. The Essex High School Marching Band was tuning up in front of the courthouse while the band from Kennedy, Toby's school, was doing the same in front of the library. The Hamilton Drum and Bugle Corps was practicing, too. Cub scouts, boy scouts, and girl scouts were everywhere. Children on bicycles wheeled in and out of the crowd, streamers flying from their handlebars. Every now and then Val caught a glimpse of Doc in his dog suit, moving from one group to the next, trying to get everyone to line up. Other Humane Society members in animal suits were scattered here and there, and some were already in place on the flatbed truck that was to serve as the float. The truck was decorated with crepe paper rosettes and big signs that said: ADOPT-A-PET — GIVE AN ANIMAL A HOME; THE ESSEX HUMANE SOCIETY NEEDS *YOU*!; and ANIMALS ARE OUR FRIENDS.

Glancing at the float, Val saw a fat pink pig huddled down near the back. It was such a good pig suit that she rode The Ghost over to take a closer look. The pig looked up, and Val found herself looking into the furious face of Lila Bascombe.

"I'll get even with you for this, Valentine Taylor, I swear I will!" Lila said from under her snout. "You did this on purpose!"

Val bit the inside of her cheek to keep from bursting into giggles. When she had controlled herself, she said, "Lila, I didn't even know you were riding on the float until Dad told me this morning. That's the honest-to-goodness truth." She couldn't resist adding, "You know, pink really is your color!"

"I *hate* you!" Lila squawked, but before she could say more, a large rabbit came over to her and handed her a pile of flyers. Val recognized George Frick.

"Here, Lila, these flyers tell all about the Society's building project. Toss 'em out when we start moving, okay?" He looked up at Val. "Hi, Vallie. Looking good up there!"

"Thanks, Mr. Frick. I like your ears," Val said. Then, with a broad grin at Lila, she urged The Ghost forward. The parade was finally about to begin.

As Val took her place in front of the boy scout color guard, she saw Doc running toward the float, pulling on his headpiece. Teddy waved frantically from the midst of his cub pack, and Val caught a glimpse of Erin and Olivia on their flower-trimmed bikes. Toby was holding Pedro by the halter; there was no way he was going to ride the burro in the parade in front of hundreds of people.

Val looked over her shoulder at Doc, waiting for the signal to proceed, but he held both arms up in the air, which she supposed meant she was to wait. Val understood the reason for the delay when she saw Miss Maggie Rafferty pedaling wildly down Main Street on her old bicycle. When Miss Maggie had taken her place in front of the Humane Society float, Doc lowered his arms. Val nodded to the color guard, and the Drum and Bugle Corps began to play a stirring march. The Ghost pranced around a little, arching his neck, and tossing his head, but Val quickly calmed him with a soothing pat on his neck. A cheer went up from the people lining the streets. The parade was under way!

Chapter
10

The grounds of Miss Maggie's big old house were filled with happy people. Everyone was caught up in the holiday spirit, enjoying all the activities, and spending money, as Mike said to Val at one point, like it was going out of style. He'd brought Ludwig with him, of course, and Pedro, who'd been getting a little jittery from all the noise and confusion, relaxed immediately when he saw his old friend.

Val, hot, sweaty, and triumphant in her Hamilton Raiders softball uniform, made her way through the crowd to the ring Toby and Mike had roped off for burro rides. People kept stopping her, shaking her hand, patting her on the back, and congratulating her on the Raiders' victory. The game had been played on the field behind Miss Maggie's house, and the Raiders had won in the ninth inning when Sarah Jones had hit a home run with the bases loaded. One of the runs she'd driven in had been Val's, but Val knew she couldn't take any credit for the victory. Sarah was the hero of the day. Still, Val was proud and happy, even though she knew that a lot of the Buccaneers wouldn't be speaking to the Raiders for a while after their defeat.

"Hey, Toby! Did you hear? We won!" she shouted, coming up to the ring.

"I heard, all right," Toby said. "And all I can say is, you girls sure were lucky!"

"What do you mean, lucky?" Val cried. "We played better, that's all."

But Toby shook his head with an infuriatingly superior smile on his face. "Those guys must have let you win," he said. "Everybody knows that boys are better athletes than girls. But congratulations, anyway. How'd you like to lead Pedro around for a while? I'd like to take a break and get some of Dad's ice cream."

When was Toby ever going to learn about equality of the sexes, Val thought, exasperated. Swallowing her annoyance, Val nodded. "Sure, go ahead. Could you bring me back a cone?"

"What flavor?"

"Any flavor, just as long as it's cold. Okay, who's next?" she said, turning to the children who were standing impatiently in line.

"Me," cried a little girl whose face was made up like a clown. "I paid that boy already." She pointed at Teddy, who was collecting money in a cigar box.

"I paid him one dollar and five cents, so can I have my ride now?"

"A dollar-five?" Val repeated, lifting the child onto Pedro's back. "But Burro rides are only a dollar."

"Yeah, but the boy said for an extra five cents I could pat him, too," said the little girl. "Let's go!"

Val rolled her eyes. Teddy was turning into a really sharp businessman, she thought as she began leading Pedro around the circle, Ludwig at her side. Teddy looked up as she passed him, absently patting Pedro's neck.

"You owe me fifteen cents, Vallie!" he shouted. "Five cents a pat, and you just patted him *three times*!"

"No way," Val said, laughing. "I work here, so I get a discount. Three for a nickel!"

"You owe me," Teddy called after her.

A little while later, Erin and Olivia came over with Jill.

"We ran out of clown makeup," Jill explained, "but we made *pots* of money."

"We just came from the fashion show," Erin added. "There weren't many people there, but Lila and her friends looked really nice. Too bad Lila's such a pain. She's very pretty."

"Yes, she is," Val agreed cheerfully. "She was the prettiest pig I ever saw!"

The four girls dissolved in giggles. Suddenly Toby tapped Val on the shoulder.

"Don't look now," he said quietly, "but here comes trouble." He nodded his head in the direction of a figure that was walking their way. Val recognized the man at once. It was Mr. Wetzel, wearing what looked like the same filthy overalls and scruffy straw hat he'd had on when she'd last seen him.

Seeing Val's expression of dismay, Erin asked, "What's wrong, Vallie?"

"Nothing. I hope," Val replied.

Toby started off with another burro rider, and Val stood where she was, hoping that Wetzel would decide to go somewhere else.

But he didn't. He kept right on coming.

"Who's that dirty-looking man, Vallie?" Erin asked.

"Just a farmer," Val said quickly. Whatever Mr. Wetzel wanted, she didn't want Erin or Olivia involved. "Jill," she said, "how about buying the girls some ice cream? My treat." She took a handful of change out of her pants pocket and thrust the money at Jill.

"Huh? Oh, sure. I could use some myself," Jill said. "Is everything okay, Val?"

"Everything's fine. 'Bye, Jill. See you later," Val said, giving her friend a little push.

Mr. Wetzel came up to her as the girls headed for the ice-cream tent. He smiled at Val, showing ugly yellow teeth. Val didn't smile back.

"Well, well. If it ain't the little vet girl," Wetzel said, hooking his thumbs in the bib of his overalls. "Looks like my burro's doing pretty good."

"Pedro's fine, thank you," Val said icily.

"You know, I gotta hand it to you and your dad," Wetzel said. "You got a lot of nerve, stealin' my burro and then makin' money off him like this, right out in broad daylight. Yep, you got some nerve."

"Pedro's not your burro anymore, Mr. Wetzel," Val said. "He belongs to Animal Inn."

"Does he, now?" Wetzel chewed on what Val assumed was a plug of tobacco. She was proved right when he spat a stream of tobacco juice into the grass at her feet. "Wonder how the law would feel about that."

Val clenched her fists. "It was the law that made you pay a fine for mistreating Pedro so badly," she said. "The law's on the side of abused animals!"

"That may be," Wetzel said. "I ain't sayin' it's not. But what I'm wonderin' is, how does the law feel about people that steals animals that don't belong to them? You say Pedro here belongs to Animal Inn. You got a bill of sale from me to your dad?"

"N-no," Val faltered. She scanned the crowd milling around, searching for Doc's dog suit, but she couldn't find it.

"Now we're gettin' somewhere," Wetzel said. "You ain't got a bill of sale 'cause I never sold that animal. That animal's mine, and now I'm gonna take him back." His shifty little eyes fell on Toby's sign that was displayed next to the ring. " 'Give This Burro a Home,' " he read aloud. "Well, that's exactly what I aim to do. I thank you kindly for breakin' him for me, and now I'm gonna take back my property."

"Toby!" Val called, and Toby, who had been continuing with the burro rides, strode over to her after handing Pedro over to Mike.

"Get out of here, Wetzel," Toby growled, making his voice as deep as he could.

"Who're you tellin' to get out of here, kid?" Wetzel asked, thrusting his jaw out next to Toby's face. "Ain't nobody taught you no manners? I got a right to be here, same as everyone else. I come to this Country Fair and I paid my admission. All I want is to get my burro back. Like I told the girl here, Pedro belongs to me, and now I'm takin' him home."

He pushed Toby aside with one dirty hand, and ducked under the rope. Mike had just lifted down the child who had been riding Pedro, and he turned to face Wetzel with narrowed eyes.

"John Wetzel, you ain't got no business here," Mike said. "And don't you lay a hand on that boy or that girl! This here donkey don't belong to you no more. You touch him and I'll bust your chops for you but good! I could beat you up when we was in school together, and I can still bust your chops now!"

116

"Oh, yeah? We'll see about that!"

Wetzel lunged for Pedro's halter, shouldering Mike aside. Mike lashed out at him, but lost his footing in the slippery grass and fell down.

The minute Wetzel latched onto Pedro, Pedro started bucking and kicking. Toby tried to restrain him, but the burro knocked him flying across the ring.

And then Ludwig sprang. Growling deep in his throat, the big German shepherd sank his teeth into Wetzel's leg.

"Get that killer dog off me!" Wetzel cried. "Help! Police!"

Mike grabbed Ludwig's collar, pulling him away. The children and their parents who were waiting for rides screamed, and Val screamed, too.

"Dad!" she cried. "Dad, help!"

Suddenly she felt a strong arm around her shoulders, and Doc was saying, "Wetzel, I'm going to break you into a million pieces!"

"You stole my burro," Wetzel whimpered, clutching his injured leg. "I'll have the law on you, see if I don't!"

"John Wetzel, stand up!"

A sharp, clear voice cut through the noise. Val saw Miss Maggie standing over Mr. Wetzel. Her face was like a thundercloud. Slowly, painfully, Mr. Wetzel struggled to his feet.

"Aw, gee, Miss Maggie . . ." he mumbled, rubbing his leg.

"John Wetzel, you have been very bad," Miss Maggie snapped. "You always were a very bad boy, but I hoped you'd outgrown your youthful meanness. Apparently you have not."

"But that's my burro," Wetzel whined. "That there vet and those kids stole him from me. Make them give him back!"

Miss Maggie glared at him.

"John Wetzel, I will pay you five hundred dollars for that burro," she said. "Will you sell him to me?"

Wetzel's beady little eyes brightened. Val could almost see the dollar signs lighting up.

"Five hundred dollars?" he echoed.

"That's what I said. In cash." Miss Maggie dug her hand into a pocket of her baggy pants and came up with a roll of bills. She glanced at Doc. "And five hundred more for the Humane Society. Don't have that much cash on me. I'll have to write a check."

"In cash?" Wetzel chomped on his chaw of tobacco and almost choked on the juice. "Five hundred dollars *in cash?*"

"Make up your mind, John Wetzel. Do you want the money or don't you?"

Wetzel looked from Pedro to Ludwig to Doc, then back to Miss Maggie.

"Sounds fair," he said at last.

Miss Maggie peeled off five one-hundred dollar bills. She held them out to him.

"The burro is mine. Go home, John Wetzel. But be advised that if I ever hear of your mistreating an animal again, I will personally make sure that you wind up in one of the shelters for homeless *people* that the town of Essex provides. How would you like to live in the Molly Pitcher Hotel, where people live who have no other homes to go to?"

Wetzel snatched the money and tucked it into the bib of his overalls. Without a word, he turned away and shoved through the crowd that had gathered.

Val flung her arms around Miss Maggie's neck.

"Oh, thank you!" she cried. "You saved Pedro's life!"

"Guess I did," Miss Maggie said. "Now I have to decide what I'm going to do with him. Got any ideas?"

"Not yet," Val said. "But I'm sure you'll come up with something!"

"Val, come here!" Toby called excitedly a week later.

"What's up, Toby?" Val was jotting down a message from a farmer who wanted Doc to come out and look at his ailing horse. "Can't you tell me about it?"

"No! You have to *see* it!"

Val came out from behind the reception desk at Animal Inn and joined Toby at the window.

"What am I supposed to be looking at?" she asked.

Then she saw. A bright, shiny cart was pulling up in the parking lot. Between the shafts was Pedro, looking fat and sassy. And on the driver's seat was Miss Maggie. Her salt-and-pepper hair was confined beneath a straw hat covered with flowers. It looked a little odd in contrast to her baggy trousers and plaid shirt.

Next to Miss Maggie on the seat was Ludwig. His long pink tongue was hanging out. It looked as though he was smiling.

As Val watched, Miss Maggie got down from the seat and lifted out a cat carrier from the back of the cart. She put the cat carrier down while she tethered Pedro to a tree, then picked it up again and marched up to the front door of Animal Inn.

Val ran to open the door.

"Brought Calico for her checkup," Miss Maggie said. "Now that I have Pedro, I don't have to depend on house calls anymore. Tell your father I'm here."

"I sure will!"

Val ran off to inform Doc of his latest patient. She was grinning from ear to ear.

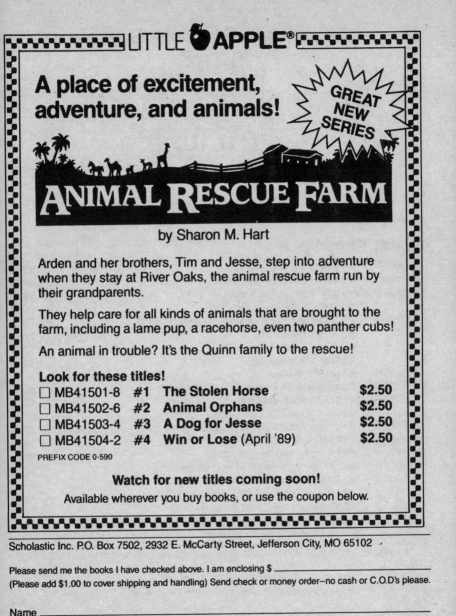